Your Movie Guide To

WESTERN

VIDEO TAPES AND DISCS

By the Editors of

VIDEO TIMES MAGAZINE

Written by Alex Gordon and the contributing editors of *Video Times* magazine, under the general editorship of Tim Lucas.

The photographs in this book are courtesy of the following studios and organizations:
Movie Star News; Warner Bros.; Cineman Syndicate; United Artists; Universal City Studios and The Malpaso Co.; MGM/UA; MCA Home Video; Columbia Pictures Industries, Inc.; Universal City Studios; Alex Gordon; Paramount Pictures.

PRINTED IN CANADA

INTRODUCTION

A dusty street with a saloon at one end and a half-built church at the other; covered wagons crossing an endless valley studded with awesome mountains; two men, one in black, one in white, facing off under a burning noonday sun—these are instantly recognizable images, made familiar all over the world by the western. Once a Saturday-matinee staple, the western has suffered a decline in popularity over the last 30 years. But perhaps with the rise of the home video market, the "Three Mesquiteers" and the "Range Busters" will soon be riding the plains again.

It's fascinating to note that the life of the western movie closely parallels the career of its greatest star, John Wayne (whose contributions are well documented on video). Wayne, too, began with B-westerns, starred in serials, hit the high tide in such classics as *Stagecoach* and *Angel and the Badman,* delivered unforgettable performances in thematically complex westerns such as *Red River* and *The Searchers*, and finally turned to comic westerns like *Rooster Cogburn* before his final performance as the cancer-stricken gunman in *The Shootist*.

Since Wayne's death, Clint Eastwood has been the only actor to make serious contributions to the western. He came to prominence as the "Man With No Name" in Sergio Leone's "Dollars" triology and later became the director of *High Plains Drifter* and *The Outlaw Josey Wales*. Only the westerns of director Sam Peckinpah have given Eastwood a run for his money, surpassing him in terms of adding to the genre, but falling far short of him in box-office returns.

This directory to the westerns available for home video viewing covers the entire history of the genre: the early classics, the cliff-hanger serials, the B-pictures, the musical-westerns, the masterpieces, and even the oddball parodies. What it may lack (out of necessity) in terms of modern heroes, it compensates for with the genre's founding fathers. So, let's get along, little dogies, back to those clear-cut, no-nonsense days when men were men, women were women, fun was fun, whiskey was a buffalo nickel, right was right and wrong never triumphed, and audiences were glad of it all.

ABILENE TOWN (1946) B/W. *Dir.:* Edwin L. Marin. *With:* Randolph Scott, Ann Dvorak, Rhonda Fleming, Lloyd Bridges. **89 mins.** No rating. Beta, VHS **($19.95).** Kartes. ★★½

A post-Civil War western in which a sheriff tries to settle a battle between the cattlemen and the homesteaders in Kansas territory. An above-average production with a good cast. Features Lloyd Bridges in an early role.

ALAMO, THE (1960) C. *Dir.:* John Wayne. *With:* John Wayne, Richard Widmark, Laurence Harvey, Richard Boone, Linda Cristal, Frankie Avalon, Chill Wills. **161 mins.** No rating. Beta, VHS **($79.95);** CED **($39.98).** CBS/Fox. ★★½

Wayne plays Davy Crockett in this star-studded, long, slow epic that culminates in a spectacular (but historically inaccurate) battle for the Alamo. Wayne produced the film and also directed (with some help from John Ford). The movie was nominated for an Oscar for Best Picture, and Wills was nominated for Best Supporting Actor. Gordon Sawyer and Fred Hynes won Oscars for Best Sound.

ALLEGHENY UPRISING (1939) B/W. *Dir.:* William Seiter. *With:* John Wayne, Claire Trevor, George Sanders, Chill Wills, Brian Donlevy. **81 mins.** No rating. Beta, VHS **($29.95).** Nostalgia Merchant. ★★½

After the success of *Stagecoach*, Wayne and Trevor were reteamed in this entertaining but sometimes slow-moving costume drama set in pre-Revolutionary War America. Wayne leads a band of colonists trying to stop a crooked merchant (Donlevy) from selling liquor, guns, and tomahawks to the Indians. However, Donlevy has finagled a safe conduct pass from the British authorities, so the men must battle the British army, too. The film's release in England was delayed, but it was finally shown under the title *The First Rebel.*

ALONG CAME JONES (1945) B/W. *Dir.:* Stuart Heisler. *With:* Gary Cooper, Loretta Young, William Demarest. **93 mins.** No rating. Beta, VHS **($59.98).** Key. ★★★

In this entertaining comic western, peaceful cowhand Cooper is mistaken for the infamous gunfighter Duryea, who is being pursued both by the law and by double-crossed outlaws. This lightweight material is expertly handled by a splendid cast, who turn it into a surprisingly involving venture. Cooper pro-

The Alamo

Along Came Jones

duced this vehicle himself, recognizing a grand opportunity to showcase his comedic gifts.

ALVAREZ KELLY (1966) C. *Dir.:* Edward Dmytryk. *With:* William Holden, Richard Widmark, Janice Rule, Victoria Shaw, Patrick O'Neal. **116 mins.** No rating. Beta, VHS **($59.95).** RCA/Columbia. ★★

A sprawling Civil War story about a Texas cattleman (Holden) who is trying to deliver his herd to a Union army commander (O'Neal). Widmark plays a Rebel leader who is determined to get the cattle for the South. Slow and not all that interesting.

AMERICAN EMPIRE (1942) B/W. *Dir.:* William McGann. *With:* Richard Dix, Leo Carrillo, Preston Foster, Frances Gifford. **82 mins.** No rating. Beta, VHS **($19.95).** Kartes. ★★★

Mexican rustlers interfere with a couple of partners who are trying to build a cattle empire. A robust, medium-scale action film with an interesting cast. Frances (*Jungle Girl*) Gifford is the female lead.

ANGEL AND THE BADMAN (1947) B/W. *Dir.:* James Edward Grant. *With:* John Wayne, Gail Russell, Harry Carey. **99 mins.** No rating. Beta, VHS **($19.95)**. Crown, Kartes, Media. ★★★

Wayne made one of his best Republic films with this modest, philosophic western, which finds the Duke persuaded to give up his gunslinging days by a loving Quaker girl

(Russell). Just as he's about to hang up his holster for good, archenemy Cabot shows up, and the score can only be settled with bullets. Wayne produced the film, and the exciting action sequences were staged and directed by renowned stuntman Yakima Canutt.

ANNIE OAKLEY (1935) B/W. *Dir.:* George Stevens. *With:* Barbara Stanwyck, Preston Foster, Melvyn Douglas, Moroni Olson, Chief Thundercloud. **90 mins.** No rating. Beta, VHS **($N/A)**. Nostalgia Merchant. ★★½

A backwoods girl becomes a sharpshooter and joins Buffalo Bill Cody's Wild West Show, where she has a stormy romance with her conceited male counterpart (Foster). Stanwyck is wonderful as the title heroine, whose life was also the basis for the hit musical *Annie Get Your Gun.* Although a bit dated, this version is an enjoyable comedy-drama about early show business.

APACHE (1954) C. *Dir.:* Robert Aldrich. *With:* Burt Lancaster, Jean Peters, John McIntire. **91 mins.** No rating. Beta, VHS **($59.98)**; CED **($19.98)**. CBS/Fox. ★★★

An Indian warrior fighting for his tribe's rights is bested by the U.S. cavalry. A moving drama with effective action sequences. Watch for Charles Buchinsky, also known as Charles Bronson. The film was coproduced by Lancaster.

APACHE ROSE (1947) B/W. *Dir.:* William Witney. *With:* Roy Rogers, Dale Evans, Olin Howard, George Meeker. **54 mins.** No rating. Beta, VHS **($24.95)**. Discount. ★★

The discovery of oil on a ranch near Las Vegas attracts a passel of crooked gamblers. Originally filmed in color, the film is available on tape only in black and white. It features Dale and the Sons of the Pioneers, but alas, no Gabby Hayes.

ARIZONA BOUND (1941) B/W. *Dir.:* Spencer Bennet. *With:* Buck Jones, Tim McCoy, Raymond Hatton. **57 mins.** No rating. Beta, VHS **($N/A)**. Video Connection. ★★★

Three lawmen come to town in disguise to expose crooks trying to grab a stagecoach franchise. The first of Monogram's popular "The Rough Riders" series, teaming western greats Buck Jones, Tim McCoy, and Raymond Hatton. Throughly enjoyable.

ARIZONA COWBOY, THE (1949) B/W. *Dir.:* R.G. Springsteen. *With:* Rex Allen, Teala Loring, Gordon Jones, Minerva Urecal. **57 mins.** No rating. Beta, VHS **($29.95).** Discount. ★★½

Rex Allen's first starring film is a pleasant mixture of action and songs. He plays a rodeo star who returns home and helps his friends break up an outlaw gang. Not one of Allen's best, but his fans won't be disappointed.

ARIZONA DAYS (1937) B/W. *Dir.:* John English. *With:* Tex Ritter, Eleanor Stewart, Snub Pollard. **52 mins.** No rating. Beta, VHS **($39.95);** Video Yesteryear. Beta, VHS **($47.95).** United. ★

This is a crudely made, mini-budget Tex Ritter vehicle with the star at his hammiest. Ritter joins a minstrel group and manages to save the show from both the bad guys and financial failure. The film is further hampered by an exceedingly rough and scratchy soundtrack.

ARIZONA RAIDERS (1965) C. *Dir.:* William Witney. *With:* Audie Murphy, Michael Dante, Buster Crabbe, Gloria Talbott. **88 mins.** No rating. Beta, VHS **($47.95).** United. ★★

A former Confederate officer joins the Arizona Rangers to fight Quantrill's Raiders. This is an enjoyable Zane Grey western with attractive players, and it provides a rare opportunity to see Crabbe in a good western lead. Reissued as *Bad Men of Arizona*.

BAD MAN OF DEADWOOD (1941) B/W. *Dir.:* Joseph Kane. *With:* Roy Rogers, George "Gabby" Hayes, Henry Brandon, Carol Adams. **54 mins.** No rating. Beta, VHS **($24.95)**. Discount. ★½

A reformed gunman joins a traveling show as a sharpshooter. This early, low-budget Rogers film features Gabby Hayes, and old timers Monte Blue and Herbert Rawlinson.

BAD MAN'S RIVER (1972) C. *Dir.:* Gene Martin. *With:* Lee Van Cleef, James Mason, Gina Lollobrigida. **89 mins.** Rated R. Beta, VHS **($59.95)**. Video Gems. ★★½

An Italian comedy-western filmed in Spain, with Van Cleef as a leader of an outlaw gang. Lollobrigida is the woman with brains who continually outwits him. A strong cast can't make up for the predictable comedy or mediocre script.

BAD MEN OF ARIZONA. See ARIZONA RAIDERS.

BARBAROSA (1982) C. *Dir.:* Fred Schepisi. *With:* Willie Nelson, Gary Busey, Danny De La Paz, Gilbert Roland. **90 mins.** Rated R. Beta, VHS **($59.98)**; CED **($19.98)**. CBS/Fox. ★★★

Willie Nelson stars as an aging desperado, with Busey as his young, high-spirited protégé. Together they experience a series of violent encounters which lead to Busey's coming of age, and Nelson's inevitable death. This low-budget western thrives on the offbeat casting of Nelson and Busey. Gilbert Roland, a veteran of many westerns from the days of silent films to contemporary cinema, is excellent as the wealthy Mexican landowner who demands the older outlaw's death. A slow-moving, but intelligent film that explores the mythology of the western and its hero.

BELLS OF ROSARITA (1945) B/W. *Dir.:* Frank McDonald. *With:* Roy Rogers, Dale Evans, George "Gabby" Hayes, Bill Elliott. **54 mins.** No rating. Beta, VHS **($24.95)**. Discount. ★★★★

During the course of filming a movie, Rogers and the Sons of the Pioneers come to the aid of Evans after bad guy Grant Withers tries to cheat her out of her circus. Lots of fun follows, with Rogers calling on his fellow western stars for help. Guests include "Wild Bill" Elliott, Allan Lane, Bob Livingston, Sunset Carson, and Don "Red" Barry. This is one of the best of Rogers' musical westerns.

Bells of Rosarita

BELOW THE BORDER (1942) B/W. *Dir.:* Howard Bretherton. *With:* Buck Jones, Tim McCoy, Raymond Hatton. **57 mins.** No rating. Beta, VHS **($24.95)**. Discount. ★★

Buck Jones pretends to be a bandit in order to round up a gang of rustlers. The story doesn't really matter—it's just another "Rough Riders" adventure. The pleasure is in seeing Jones, Tim McCoy, and Raymond Hatton work together.

BETWEEN MEN (1935) B/W. *Dir.:* Robert N. Bradbury. *With:* Johnny Mack Brown, Beth Marlon. **59 mins.** No rating. Beta, VHS **($24.95)**. Discount. ★★★

One of Johnny Mack Brown's best low-budget Supreme westerns, with William Farnum as the outlaw father who believes his son is dead. A strong plot and fine scenery make this very satisfactory entertainment.

BILLY THE KID RETURNS (1938) B/W. *Dir.:* Joseph Kane. *With:* Roy Rogers, Smiley Burnette, Lynn Roberts, Morgan Wallace. **60 mins.** No rating. Beta, VHS **($24.95)**. Discount. ★★½

In his second starring role, Roy Rogers poses as the famous outlaw in order to tame a lawless town. The film features good action, Smiley Burnette as the sidekick, and Fred Kohler as the evil villain. Check this one out if you're interested in Rogers' early work.

BILLY THE KID VS. DRACULA (1966) C. *Dir.:* William Beaudine. *With:* Chuck Courtney, John Carradine, Melinda Plowman, Harry Carey, Jr. **73 mins.** No rating. Beta, VHS **($49.95)**. Video Yesteryear. ★★

Count Dracula journeys to the Old West and masquerades as the uncle of a beautiful ranch owner, whom he wants to whisk away and make his bride in the land of the undead. A reformed Billy the Kid (her foreman and fiancé) suspects the old man and does his best to stop him. Entertaining fluff which pits the two lengendary characters against each other.

BLAZING ARROWS. See FIGHTING CARAVANS

BLAZING SADDLES (1974) C. *Dir.:* Mel Brooks. *With:* Cleavon Little, Gene Wilder, Madeline Kahn, Harvey Korman, Slim Pickens, Alex Karras. **90 mins.** Rated R. Beta, VHS **($49.95)**; Laser **($29.98)**; CED **($19.98)**. Warner. ★★★

Mel Brooks' spoof of Hollywood westerns features Little as a black sheriff and Karras as a brute who punches out horses. This parody was so on target that many viewers haven't been able to take the genre seriously since.

BLOCKED TRAIL, THE (1943) B/W. *Dir.:* Elmer Clifton. *With:* Bob Steele, Tom Tyler, Jimmie Dodd, Helen Deverell. **56 mins.** No rating. Beta, VHS **($29.95)**. Discount. ★½

The Three Mesquiteers are accused of murdering a miner in this rather weak entry in the series featuring the cowboy trio. Other entries have better production values and are much more action-packed. The viewer is better off skipping this one.

BLOOD ON THE MOON (1948) B/W. *Dir.:* Robert Wise. *With:* Robert Mitchum, Barbara Bel Geddes, Robert Preston, Walter Brennan. **88 mins.** No rating. Beta, VHS **($29.95).** Nostalgia Merchant. ★★★

A tough cowboy (Mitchum) gets caught up in a range war between cattlemen and farmers. An effective, hard-hitting drama from director Wise. Preston (*The Music Man, Victor/Victoria*), Bel Geddes, and Mitchum deliver stunning performances. Highly recommended.

BLUE CANADIAN ROCKIES (1952) B/W. *Dir.:* George Archainbaud. *With:* Gene Autry, Pat Buttram, Gail Davis. **58 mins.** No rating. Beta, VHS **($34.98)**. Blackhawk. ★★½

Autry's boss sends him to Canada to save his daughter from marrying a fortune hunter. Gene discovers the daughter is operating a dude ranch and wild-game preserve. However, when some mysterious killings occur, Gene and comic sidekick Pat Buttram volunteer to investigate. The Cass County Boys, well-known at the time for their appearances on Autry's *Melody Ranch* radio program, provide the catchy musical numbers. An average Autry oater.

BLUE STEEL (1934) B/W. *Dir.:* N/A. *With:* John Wayne, George Hayes, Yakima Canutt, Eleanor Hunt. **55 mins.** No rating. Beta, VHS **($19.95).** Kartes, Sony, Spotlite. ★★

Gold fever can drive men to evil. Outlaws discover gold deposits in the land beneath a quiet little town. Honest ranchers are forced out or murdered until the Duke arrives to bring the ruthless criminals to justice. The film features George Hayes in his pre-"Gabby" days. (Sony's tapes are in Beta Hi-Fi and VHS Hi-Fi.)

BOILING POINT (1932) B/W. *Dir.:* N/A. *With:* Hoot Gibson. **60 mins.** No rating. Beta, VHS **($39.95)**. United ★★½

A breezy Hoot Gibson western that combines action and comedy. Gibson was a big silent star who kept his career going into the early forties. His independent films of the thirties (of which this is one) are funny and nonviolent—Gibson rarely carries a gun.

BOOTS AND SADDLES (1937) B/W. *Dir.:* Joseph Kane. *With:* Gene Autry, Bill Elliott, Smiley Burnette, Judith Allen. **59 mins.** No rating. Beta, VHS **($34.98).** Blackhawk. ★★★½

A British youngster, an heir to a ranch, learns to appreciate the outdoor life with the help of ranch foreman Autry. Autry is raising horses for a cavalry regiment and falls in love with the colonel's daughter. This large-scale, early Republic western offers romance, comedy, and action, climaxing in a thrilling horse race. Bill Elliott, who later became famous as "Wild Bill" Elliott, plays a bad guy.

BORROWED TROUBLE (1948) B/W. *Prod.:* William Boyd. *With:* Hopalong Cassidy (William Boyd), Rand Brooks, Andy Clyde. **58 mins.** No rating. Beta, VHS **($59.95)**. Blackhawk. ★★

This is one of the many films from the Hopalong Cassidy series popular during the 1930s and 1940s. Here Hoppy and his pals are involved in a dispute which pits reading, writing, and arithmetic against saloons, rabble-rousing, and gambling. A later Hopalong Cassidy film, with shoddier production values than the earlier ones.

BRONCO BILLY (1980) C. *Dir.:* Clint Eastwood. *With:* Clint Eastwood, Sondra Locke, Geoffrey Lewis, Sam Bottoms, Dan Vadis, Scatman Crothers. **118 mins.** Rated PG. Beta, VHS **($59.95);** CED **($19.98)**. Warner. ★★★

A charming, low-key comedy about a self-styled cowboy who runs a ragtag Wild West show featuring a small troupe of offbeat performers (Crothers, Vadis, Bottoms). This unusual depiction of the western hero makes for a slightly uneven film, particularly with Eastwood in the title role, but it is still humorous and entertaining.

BUCKSKIN FRONTIER (1943) B/W. *Dir.:* Lesley Selander. *With:* Richard Dix, Jane Wyatt, Lee J. Cobb. **75 mins.** No rating. Beta, VHS **($N/A)**. Independent United Distributors. ★★★

The building of the railroad results in a conflict between the builders and some outlaws. A rip-roaring western with fine action and a good cast. From the producer of the Hopalong Cassidy films.

BUFFALO BILL AND THE INDIANS, OR SITTING BULL'S HISTORY LESSON (1976) C. *Dir.:* Robert Altman. *With:* Paul Newman, Joel Grey, Kevin McCarthy, Burt Lancaster, Geraldine Chaplin, Harvey Keitel, Will Sampson. **120 mins.** Rated PG. Beta, VHS **($59.98)**. Key. ★★½

An offbeat study of the legendary Buffalo Bill that portrays him as a product of media hype rather than an honest-to-goodness cowboy. Newman gives a strong performance in the lead role, but the rambling story soon loses momentum.

BUFFALO STAMPEDE (1933) B/W. *Dir.:* Henry Hathaway. *With:* Randolph Scott, Harry Carey, Judith Allen, Larry "Buster" Crabbe. **60 mins.** No rating. Beta, VHS **($N/A)**. Video Connection. ★★★

A buffalo hunter romances an outlaw's daughter and becomes involved in a variety of adventures involving Indians and buffaloes. A superior Paramount western that includes stock footage from the spectacular silent version. The strong cast includes Buster Crabbe, Noah Beery, Harry Carey, and Barton MacLane. (aka THE THUNDERING HERD.)

BUTCH CASSIDY AND THE SUNDANCE KID (1969) C. *Dir.:* George Roy Hill. *With:* Paul Newman, Robert Redford, Katharine Ross, Strother Martin, Henry Jones, Cloris Leachman, Ted Cassidy, Kenneth Mars. **112 mins.** Rated PG. Beta, VHS **($69.98);** Laser **($29.98);** CED **($19.98)**. CBS/Fox. ★★★★

A superb, Academy Award-winning western-comedy with Newman and Redford as a pair of luckless bank robbers trying to keep one step ahead of the law. The pair's escapades alternate between the humorous and the tragic, leading to a rather grim conclusion. Based on the actual exploits of the historical characters, the script by William Goldman is both witty and touching. Best remembered for the exciting stuntwork and the hit song "Raindrops Keep Falling on My Head."

CAHILL—U.S. MARSHAL (1973) C. *Dir.:* Andrew V. McLaglen. *With:* John Wayne, George Kennedy, Gary Grimes, Clay O'Brien, Neville Brand. **103 mins.** Rated PG. Beta, VHS **($59.95).** Warner. ★★

John Wayne plays a marshal who faces a dilemma when his two sons (Grimes and O'Brien) decide to lead a life of lawlessness. He discovers they are involved in the bank robbery he is investigating. When the boys try to go straight, they run into resistance from their old gang, led by villain Kennedy. Although well crafted by old pros, the movie is only occasionally entertaining and often indulges in overly sentimental preachiness. Not one of the Duke's better efforts.

Butch Cassidy and the Sundance Kid

California Joe

CALIFORNIA JOE (1943) B/W. *Dir.:* Spencer Bennet. *With:* Don Barry, Lynn Merrick, Helen Talbot, Wally Vernon. **55 mins.** No rating. Beta, VHS **($29.95).** Discount. ★★

A Union officer pretends to be an outlaw in order to foil a crooked empire builder. A reliable Republic action formula, with Lynn Merrick as the attractive heroine. Recommended to Don Barry fans.

CALLING WILD BILL ELLIOTT/SANTA FE SADDLEMATES (1943/1945) B/W. *Dir.:* Spencer Bennet/Thomas Carr. *With:* Bill Elliott, George "Gabby" Hayes, Anne Jeffries, Herbert Heyes/Sunset Carson, Linda Stirling, Roy Barcroft. **109 mins.** No rating. Beta, VHS **($N/A).** Nostalgia Merchant. ★★★/★★★★½

Calling Wild Bill Elliott, the first of Wild Bill's Republic westerns, is a superior action picture with hard riding, lots of fighting, and no-nonsense support from Gabby Hayes and Anne Jeffries. It's highly recommended to Elliott fans.

Santa Fe Saddlemates packs three big fist fights in its first few minutes. An action-filled Sunset Carson western, it gives you a good idea why Republic Studio was the best of the "B"s. Linda Stirling, "Queen of the Republic Serials," costars with

Carson and makes a charming western heroine. This is a must for all B-western fans.

CALL OF THE CANYON (1942) B/W. *Dir.:* Joseph Santley. *With:* Gene Autry, Smiley Burnette, Ruth Terry, Sons of the Pioneers. **71 mins.** No rating. Beta, VHS **($34.98).** Blackhawk. ★★★½

A cattle stampede, a stolen train, and the crooked agent of a meat packing company cause plenty of trouble for rancher Autry. This is an elaborate Autry special with many good plot twists and great songs. Gene on horseback chases a plane in the climax!

CARSON CITY KID (1940) B/W. *Dir.:* Joseph Kane. *With:* Roy Rogers, Bob Steele, George "Gabby" Hayes, Pauline Moore. **54 mins.** No rating. Beta, VHS **($N/A).** Nostalgia Merchant, Video Connection. ★★

This slow, undistinguished Rogers film is helped by the presence of Steele and Noah Beery, Jr. The melodramatic script, about a stage robber who is reformed by love, is based on a story by director Kane. The movie provides an atypical role for Rogers, but Gabby Hayes, as usual, plays the faithful comic sidekick.

CAT BALLOU (1965) C. *Dir.:* Elliot Silverstein. *With:* Jane Fonda, Lee Marvin, Michael Callan, Dwayne Hickman, Tom Nardini. **96 mins.** No rating. Beta, VHS **($64.95);** CED **($19.98).** RCA/Columbia. ★★★

Schoolteacher Fonda becomes an outlaw when ruthless businessmen kill her father and try to take his land away from her. Marvin is marvelous in a dual role as twin brothers—one an evil, cruel killer with no nose, the other a washed-up, drunken ex-gunfighter. He won a Best Actor Oscar for his work. This western spoof has some hilarious moments, but it is probably more appealing to general audiences than to fans of the genre. Nat King Cole and Stubby Kaye serve as the musical narrators.

CATTLE QUEEN OF MONTANA (1954) C. *Dir.:* Allan Dwan. *With:* Barbara Stanwyck, Ronald Reagan, Gene Evans, Lance Fuller, Jack Elam. **88 mins.** No rating. Beta, VHS **($59.95).** Buena Vista. ★★½

Rustlers kill a cattle baron and try to steal his land. The

rancher's feisty daughter (Stanwyck) fights them off with the help of a friendly Indian and a lawman who masquerades as a gunfighter. Although predictable, this one is worth seeing both for the scenery and for the Stanwyck/Reagan combination.

CHISUM (1970) C. *Dir.:* Andrew V. McLaglen. *With:* John Wayne, Forrest Tucker, Ben Johnson, Christopher George. **111 mins.** Rated G. Beta, VHS **($59.95).** Warner. ★★★

Wayne plays a cattle baron fighting corruption in this sprawling action yarn. He's helped in his feud with rival Tucker by Billy the Kid (Geoffrey Deuel) and Pat Garrett (Glenn Corbett). It's very good entertainment, with Wayne in top form. The movie was filmed in Mexico and directed by Victor McLaglen's son.

CIRCLE OF DEATH (1936) B/W. *Dir.:* J. Frank Glendon. *With:* Montie Montana, Yakima Canutt. **55 mins.** No rating. Beta, VHS **($29.95).** Video Dimensions. ★

A baby survives an Indian massacre, and grows up to fight the bad guys who want to steal his land. A very cheaply made, crude, independent western, only recommended to those who want to see Montie Montana in a leading role. Watch for Princess Ah-Tee-Ha.

CODE OF THE PRAIRIE (1944) B/W. *Dir.:* Spencer Bennet. *With:* Sunset Carson, Smiley Burnette, Peggy Stewart, Weldon Heyburn. **56 mins.** No rating. Beta, VHS **(29.95).** Discount. ★★½

A newspaper editor's murder is the focal point of this Republic action western. It's one of a series of films costarring Sunset Carson and Smiley Burnette, with Peggy Stewart the leading lady. Reliable B-western fare.

COLORADO (1940) B/W. *Dir.:* Joseph Kane. *With:* Roy Rogers, George "Gabby" Hayes, Pauline Moore, Milburn Stone. **54 mins.** No rating. Beta, VHS **($N/A).** Nostalgia Merchant. ★★

One of Rogers' lesser westerns. The action is both scarce and sluggish, and the good guys vs. the bad guys plot is dull and tired. Pretty routine stuff. Milburn Stone later went on to fame as Doc Adams on the long-running TV series *Gunsmoke.*

COMANCHEROS, THE (1961) C. *Dir.:* Michael Curtiz. *With:* John Wayne, Stuart Whitman, Ina Balin, Lee Marvin, Nehemiah

Persoff, Bruce Cabot, Michael Ansara. **108 mins.** No rating. Beta, VHS **($49.98);** CED **($19.98).** CBS/Fox. ★★★

A Texas Ranger (Wayne) and his dashing gambler prisoner (Whitman) infiltrate the Comancheros, an outlaw gang that is supplying liquor and weapons to the Comanches. This fast, action-filled western makes highly satisfying entertainment. Western veteran Bob Steele has a bit part, as does Wayne's son Patrick; Wayne's daughter Aissa also appears briefly.

COME ON, COWBOYS (1937) B/W. *Dir.:* Joseph Kane. *With:* Bob Livingston, Ray Corrigan, Max Terhune, Yakima Canutt. **54 mins.** No rating. Beta, VHS **($N/A).** Nostalgia Merchant. ★★★

An action-packed western with the original Three Mesquiteers—Livingston, Corrigan, and Terhune—coming to the aid of an old circus comrade. A grand entertainment with a rousing score, this film is one of the best in the series.

COME ON, RANGERS (1938) B/W *Dir.:* Joseph Kane. *With:* Roy Rogers, Mary Hart (Lynn Roberts). **56 mins.** No rating. Beta, VHS **($24.95).** Discount. ★★½

A very entertaining early Rogers film in which the Rangers disband—with dismaying results. The interesting cast includes Raymond Hatton, J. Farrel MacDonald, and Republic's original Lone Ranger, Lee Powell. The movie is more action-oriented than Rogers' later films.

COME ON, TARZAN (1932) B/W. *Dir.:* Alan James. *With:* Ken Maynard. **60 mins.** No rating. Beta, VHS **($24.95).** Discount. ★★★

Tarzan (the horse, not the ape-man) is mistaken for a killer, and his innocence must be proven. This primitive, old-fashioned Maynard western is packed with exciting stunts and action. A good one for his fans.

COWBOY AND THE SENORITA, THE (1944) B/W. *Dir.:* Joseph Kane. *With:* Roy Rogers, John Hubbard, Dale Evans. **56 mins.** No rating. Beta, VHS **($24.95).** Discount. ★★★

Dale Evans plays the senorita in her first of 20 films with Roy Rogers. Here, Rogers helps her and little Mary Lee fend off the bad guys who are trying to grab their gold mine. A good example of mid-forties Rogers, with Guinn "Big Boy" Williams and Fuzzy Knight contributing to the fun.

COWBOYS, THE (1972) C. *Dir.:* Mark Rydell. *With:* John Wayne, Roscoe Lee Browne, Bruce Dern, Colleen Dewhurst, Slim Pickens, Sarah Cunningham, Robert Carradine. **128 mins.** Rated PG. Beta, VHS **($59.95).** Warner. ★★½

John Wayne stars as a cattleman who, desperate for a crew for his roundup, recruits 11 young boys to do the job. Wayne gives one of his best later performances in this well-produced but quite violent movie.

COW TOWN (1950) B/W. *Dir.:* John English. *With:* Gene Autry, Gail Davis, Harry Shannon, Jock O'Mahoney. **70 mins.** No rating. Beta, VHS **($34.98).** Blackhawk. ★★★½

Autry persuades some ranchers to import barbed wire, an event leading to a string of mysterious deaths. An elaborate production and offbeat plot make this compelling viewing. One of Gene's best.

DAKOTA (1945) B/W. *Dir.:* Joseph Kane. *With:* John Wayne, Vera Hruba Ralston, Walter Brennan, Ward Bond, Mike Mazurki, George "Gabby" Hayes. **82 mins.** No rating. Beta, VHS **($39.95).** Republic. ★★½

Wheat farmers are in conflict with crooked land speculators who want to take the farmers' land and make enormous profits when the railroad comes through. Wayne, of course, comes to the farmers' rescue. Ralston plays Wayne's wife in this, one of her few successful films. (In real life, Ralston was the wife of Republic boss Herbert J. Yates, who gave her films bigger budgets and better production values than most of the studio's output.) This is an entertaining actioner, with solid performances and a predictable plot.

DAKOTA INCIDENT (1956) C. *Dir.:* Lewis Foster. *With:* Dale Robertson, Linda Darnell, John Lund, Ward Bond. **88 mins.** No rating. Beta, VHS **($39.95).** Republic. ★

Stagecoach passengers try to hold off an Indian attack in this slow, dull imitation of the classic *Stagecoach* (see review). Robertson and Lund are uninteresting leads and fail to create any excitement or tension. A minor effort—pass this one up.

DANIEL BOONE (1936) B/W. *Dir.:* David Howard. *With:* George O'Brien, Heather Angel, John Carradine. **80 mins.** No rating. Beta, VHS **($19.95).** Kartes. ★★

The famous scout Daniel Boone leads a band of settlers beyond the Cumberland mountains to Kentucky in 1775. This slow B-western has its moments, and benefits greatly from Carradine's wonderfully enthusiastic performance as the villainous half-breed Simon Girty.

DARK COMMAND, THE (1940) B/W. *Dir.:* Raoul Walsh. *With:* John Wayne, Claire Trevor, Walter Pidgeon, Roy Rogers, George "Gabby" Hayes. **95 mins.** No rating. Beta, VHS **($39.95).** Republic. ★★★½

Quantrill's Raiders pillage the post-Civil War Kansas countryside. Walter Pidgeon plays Quantrill, the ex-Confederate captain turned outlaw who threatens to take over the territory. Wayne plays the marshal elected to stop him. This is a slam-bang, big-budget Republic feature, with a fine cast and lots of action. It's highly recommended.

The Dark Command

Destry Rides Again

DAWN ON THE GREAT DIVIDE (1942) B/W. *Dir.:* Howard Bretherton. *With:* Buck Jones, Tim McCoy, Raymond Hatton, Mona Barrie. **57 mins.** No rating. Beta, VHS **($19.95).** Kartes. ★★

A wagon train heads west through some perilous Indian territory in this Monogram production, which features a superior cast but is hampered by a slow-moving, familiar plot. This was Buck Jones' last film prior to his death in 1942 in a Boston nightclub fire. The movie makes interesting viewing for Buck Jones fans, but is not of much interest to anyone else.

DAWN RIDER, THE (1935) B/W. *Dir.:* Robert N. Bradbury. *With:* John Wayne, Marion Burns, Yakima Canutt, Reed Howes. **60**

mins. No rating. Beta, VHS **($19.95).** Sony, Spotlite. ★★

Wayne witnesses his father's murder by robbers. He vows to track down the killers and bring them to justice. While on their trail, Wayne is shot by the desperadoes and badly wounded. He is nursed back to health by the beautiful Burns and manages to nail the evil murderers. A routine, predictable, but enjoyable, actioner. (Sony's tapes are available in Beta Hi-Fi or VHS Hi-Fi.)

DEEP IN THE HEART OF TEXAS (1942) B/W. *Dir.:* Elmer Clifton. *With:* Johnny Mack Brown, Tex Ritter. **57 mins.** No rating. Beta, VHS **($24.95).** Discount. ★★½

Two well-known and well-loved cowboy stars are featured together in this delightful Texas tale. Brown was at the peak of his career when this film was made and was one of the highest paid western stars. Ritter at this time was known as "America's Most Beloved Cowboy." Should not be missed by fans of B-westerns.

DESERT TRAIL, THE (1935) B/W. *Dir.:* Cullen Lewis (Lew Collins). *With:* John Wayne, Eddie Chandler, Mary Kornman. **57 mins.** No rating. Beta, VHS **($19.95).** Kartes, Sony, Spotlite. ★½

Cowboys Wayne and Chandler clash over a girl. The friends compete in a rodeo for the first-place trophy, the prize money, and the girl—"Our Gang's" Mary Kornman. However, the romantic duel is interrupted when Wayne goes off into the desert to trail a band of robbers. This is a bad remake of Bob Steele's *The Ridin' Fool*, which wasn't very good itself. Why did Monogram bother with a remake? (Sony's tapes are available in Beta Hi-Fi and VHS HI-Fi.)

DESTRY RIDES AGAIN (1939) B/W. *Dir.:* George Marshall. *With:* James Stewart, Marlene Dietrich, Brian Donlevy, Charles Winninger, Mischa Auer, Una Merkel. **94 mins.** No rating. Beta, VHS **($N/A).** MCA. ★★★★

A raucous, action-filled, totally enjoyable classic western. James Stewart shines as a peace-loving sheriff who decides to clean up a corrupt, rowdy frontier town. Marlene Dietrich is unforgettable as the dance-hall girl he becomes involved with. Her performance of the song "See What the Boys in the Back Room Will Have" is the highlight of this excellent film.

DEVIL'S PLAYGROUND, THE (1946) B/W. *Dir.:* George Archainbaud. *With:* Hopalong Cassidy (William Boyd), Andy Clyde, Rand Brooks. **65 mins.** No rating. Beta, VHS **($39.95).** Buena Vista. ★★½

A better than average Hopalong Cassidy western, with Hoppy and his sidekicks desperately searching for hidden gold in a mysterious canyon known as the "Devil's Playground." The trail gets even hotter after a map and a message are discovered scrawled on a rock in a dead man's blood.

DJANGO (1976) C. *Dir.:* Giuseppe Annis. *With:* Franco Nero, Loredana Nusciak. **90 mins.** No rating. Beta, VHS **($59.95).** Sagebrush. ★★

An Italian western featuring Nero in the title role as a mysterious stranger who rides into a small Mexican border town with a girl, a Gatling gun, and a coffin. The stranger is then thrown in the middle of a war between two rival gangs of bandits. Nero is featured in one of his many action roles in this fairly violent western.

DODGE CITY (1939) C. *Dir.:* Michael Curtiz. *With:* Errol Flynn, Olivia de Havilland, Ann Sheridan, Bruce Cabot, Frank McHugh, Alan Hale. **104 mins.** No rating. Beta, VHS **($49.98)**; Laser **($34.98).** CBS/Fox. ★★★½

Midway between *The Charge of the Light Brigade* and *The Adventures of Robin Hood,* the Flynn/de Havilland/Curtiz triumverate made this near-definitive thirties western, casting Flynn as a dashing cattleman who accepts the office of sheriff, deals the bad guys their due, and makes the town safe for the homesteaders. An uncanny translation of the swashbuckler formula to the western milieu, with Curtiz's reliable visual richness and knack for flamboyant staging fully apparent, especially during the justifiably famous barroom brawl sequence.

DON AMIGO/STAGE TO CHINO (1950/1940) B/W. *Dir.:* NA/Edward Kelly. *With:* Duncan Renaldo, Leo Carrillo/George O'Brien, Virginia Vale, Roy Barcroft. **122 mins.** No rating. Beta, VHS **($34.95).** RKO. ★½

Don Amigo is the last of the Duncan Renaldo/Leo Carrillo Cisco Kid westerns, and is a minor-scale effort not to be compared with Fox's Cisco Kid films of the thirties and forties. The RKO videotape contains a unique added attraction—a prologue narrated by Renaldo highlighting the history of the cinema's "Don Quixote of the West."

Stage to Chino is a good RKO George O'Brien western in which the star plays a postal agent battling to get the mail through on time. Virginia Vale does a good job as leading lady.

DON'T FENCE ME IN (1945) B/W. *Dir.:* John English. *With:* Roy Rogers, George "Gabby" Hayes, Dale Evans. **56 mins.** No rating. Beta, VHS **($N/A).** Nostalgia Merchant. ★★★½

A girl reporter tries to get the inside story about the death of a colorful desperado. This top-flight Rogers vehicle combines good action and compelling songs, and the excellent cast includes Dale Evans, Gabby Hayes, Bob Livingston, Marc Lawrence, Bob Nolan, and the Sons of the Pioneers. The movie was inspired by Cole Porter's hit song of the same title.

DOWN DAKOTA WAY (1949) B/W. *Dir.:* William Witney. *With:* Roy Rogers, Dale Evans, Roy Barcroft, Montie Montana, Pat Brady, Foy Willing. **67 mins.** No rating. Beta, VHS **($29.95).** Republic. ★★★

Roy Rogers investigates a veterinarian's murder and uncovers a plot to sell diseased cattle to meat packers. This big-budget film features good action and a fine cast of supporting players. The Riders of the Purple Sage are also featured and add to the fine musical entertainment.

DOWN MEXICO WAY (1941) B/W. *Dir.:* Joseph Santley. *With:* Gene Autry, Smiley Burnette, Fay McKenzie, Duncan Renaldo, Eddie Dean. **78 mins.** No rating. Beta, VHS **($34.98).** Blackhawk. ★★★½

A group of crooks pose as Hollywood producers, fleece the citizens of the small town Sage City out of their savings, and head for Mexico to repeat the scheme. Autry and Smiley head south to help their friends get their money back, and encounter bandits, romance, and adventure along the way. One of Autry's best big-budget movies—terrific entertainment. Songs featured include "Down Mexico Way," "South of the Border," and "Beer Barrel Polka."

DRUM BEAT (1954) C. *Dir.:* Delmer Daves. *With:* Alan Ladd, Audrey Dalton, Charles Bronson, Marisa Pavan. **111 mins.** No rating. Beta, VHS **($54.95).** United. ★★

Drum Beat

Durango Valley Raiders

An Indian fighter (Ladd) risks his life to negotiate a peace treaty with a renegade Indian. This mild western features the fine Irish actress Audrey Dalton as an Indian girl. Charles Bronson plays the Modoc Indian chief—his first major role under the name Bronson rather than his real name, Buchinsky.

DRUM TAPS (1933) B/W. *Dir.:* J.P. McGowan. *With:* Ken Maynard, Dorothy Dix, Junior Coughlin. **55 mins.** No rating. Beta, VHS **($29.95).** Video Dimensions. ★★½

A Boy Scout troop helps Maynard round up the bad guys in this pleasant, early independent film. Ken's brother Kermit makes an appearance—he had his own series later. Enjoyable for Maynard fans.

DUDE RANGER, THE (1934) B/W. *Dir.:* Edward F. Cline. *With:* George O'Brien, Irene Hervey, Syd Saylor. **58 mins.** No rating. Beta, VHS **($29.95).** Video Dimensions. ★★

An Easterner inherits a piece of land, and comes west to claim it. Based on a Zane Grey story, this mild independent western is not up to the standards of O'Brien's Fox or RKO films, and is only for staunch O'Brien fans. The James Mason listed in the cast credits is a silent film actor, not the British star.

DURANGO VALLEY RAIDERS (1938) B/W. *Dir.:* Sam Newfield. *With:* Bob Steele, Louise Stanley. **55 mins.** No rating. Beta, VHS **($29.95).** Discount. ★★½

Although Bob Steele's films were usually low-budget efforts, they were carefully made, packed with action, and had interesting stories. In fact, the star's movies were often written and directed by his father, Robert N. Bradbury. Steele was one of the most athletic of the western stars, and did all his own stunts, including riding and fighting. This is a good example of his work.

DYNAMITE PASS (1950) B/W. *Dir.:* Lew Landers. *With:* Tim Holt, Richard Martin, Lynn Roberts, John Dehner, Denver Pyle. **61 mins.** No rating. Beta, VHS **($N/A).** Nostalgia Merchant. ★★½

A group of cattlemen tries to stop the railroad from building through their territory. A typical RKO western, the movie boasts superior production and action. The interesting cast includes Lynn Roberts, Cleo Moore, Regis Toomey, and Robert Shayne.

EAGLE'S BROOD, THE (1935) B/W. *Dir.:* Howard Bretherton. *With:* Hopalong Cassidy (William Boyd), James Ellison, William Farnum, George "Gabby" Hayes. **59 mins.** No rating. Beta, VHS **($25.00).** Cumberland. ★★★

In the second film of the popular Hopalong Cassidy series, Hoppy promises an outlaw that he will find his grandson. Fine scenery and a rousing action climax with the Bar 20 boys coming to the rescue make this a superior Paramount western.

EL DORADO (1967) C. *Dir.:* Howard Hawks. *With:* John Wayne, Robert Mitchum, James Caan, Arthur Hunnicutt, Ed Asner, Christopher George, Michele Carey, Charlene Holt. **126 mins.** No rating. Beta, VHS **($49.95);** CED **($29.95).** Paramount. ★★★½

A great, ripsnorting film, in which a tough, old gunfighter (Wayne) helps a drunken sheriff (Mitchum) fight the bad guys who are planning to break a prisoner out of jail. The good guys get some questionable assistance from ancient geezer Hunnicutt and from Caan, a cocky kid who can't shoot. A thoroughly entertaining Hawks epic, the movie is a loose remake of *Rio Bravo* (see review), which was also directed by Hawks and starred Wayne. It doesn't quite measure up to its predecessor, but there are lots of special touches and top-notch performances by Mitchum and Wayne. Asner, however, seems out of place as a western villain.

ELECTRIC HORSEMAN, THE (1979) C. *Dir.:* Sydney Pollack. *With:* Robert Redford, Jane Fonda, Valerie Perrine, Willie Nelson, John Saxon. **120 mins.** Rated PG. Beta, VHS **($79.95);** Laser **($29.98);** CED **($19.98).** MCA. ★★★

Redford stars as a washed-up rodeo star who sells out by promoting breakfast cereal. Fonda plays a TV reporter who follows Redford through the Rockies after he rebels against the system and kidnaps a multimillion dollar racehorse. Good entertainment.

EYES OF TEXAS (1948) B/W. *Dir.:* William Witney. *With:* Roy Rogers, Lynne Roberts, Andy Devine, Nana Bryant. **54 mins.** No rating. Beta, VHS **($N/A).** Video Connection. ★½

A pack of trained attack dogs terrorize innocent victims. This bloody, violent film is available in a drastically shortened video version—the original 70-minute length has been cut to 54 minutes. Nana Bryant plays the villainess who is trying to grab the valuable land with the help of her vicious dogs. Lynne Roberts and Andy Devine provide a touch of romance and comedy. (This movie is also available from Nostalgia Merchant as a double bill with *Helldorado*.)

FAR FRONTIER, THE. See TRIGGER JR./THE FAR FRONTIER.

FAST BULLETS (1944) B/W. *Dir.:* Henri Samuels (Harry S. Webb). *With:* Tom Tyler, Rex Lease, Robert Walker, William Gould. **52 mins.** No rating. Beta, VHS **($24.95).** Discount. ★★

Tom Tyler fans will enjoy his shy but sincere personality in this very low-budget western from Reliable Pictures. The production values are crude, and the action is simple. The standard plot pits Tyler against a criminal gang.

FIGHTING CARAVANS (1931) B/W. *Dir.:* Otto Brower and David Burton. *With:* Gary Cooper, Lili Damita, Ernest Torrence. **80 mins.** No rating. Beta, VHS **($49.95).** Video Yesteryear. ★

Wagon scout Cooper is hired to bring a group of homesteaders through perilous Indian country to California. A beautiful French girl (Damita) causes complications along the way, but Coop manages to deliver the settlers safely. Based on a Zane Grey novel, this is a slow, dated reworking of the silent classic *Covered Wagon*. Despite Cooper's rugged appeal, he can't overcome the tired script. The movie is only for those interested in the cast of character actors, which includes Tully Marshall, Eugene Pallette, Syd Saylor, Charles Winninger, Chief John Big Tree, Jane Darwell, and Iron Eyes Cody.

FIGHTING KENTUCKIAN, THE (1949) B/W. *Dir.:* George Waggner. *With:* John Wayne, Vera Hruba Ralston, Philip Dorn, Oliver Hardy. **100 mins.** No rating. Beta, VHS **($39.95).** Republic. ★★½

A French general's daughter is in love with a tough frontiersman who is busy battling land grabbers. This entertaining Republic upper-budget western is set during the War of 1812. The interesting cast includes Hardy, making one of his rare appearances without Stan Laurel, as Wayne's sidekick.

FIGHTING TROOPER, THE (1934) B/W. *Dir.:* Ray Taylor. *With:* Kermit Maynard, Barbara Worth, Walter Miller, LeRoy Mason. **57 mins.** No rating. Beta, VHS **($29.95).** Video Dimensions. ★★

Kermit Maynard's first starring talkie has him posing as a trapper in order to solve the murder of a friend. It's worthwhile viewing if you are a fan of this personable star.

FIRST REBEL, THE. See ALLEGHENY UPRISING.

FISTFUL OF DOLLARS, A (1966) C. *Dir.:* Sergio Leone. *With:* Clint Eastwood, Gian Maria Volonte, Marianne Koch, Mario Brega. **96 mins.** No rating. Beta, VHS **($59.95);** CED **($19.95).** CBS/Fox. ★★½

This Italian spaghetti western was shot in 1964, but its American release was delayed until 1966. The movie caused a big stir, influencing the genre for years, and brought attention and acclaim to its director and cowriter, Leone. Eastwood's portrayal of the mysterious "Man With No Name" made him an international star. The film is based on the Japanese samurai classic *Yojimbo* directed by Akira Kurosawa. A violent, nihilistic view of the West, it is recommended to action buffs and Eastwood fans.

FLAME OF THE BARBARY COAST (1945) B/W. *Dir.:* Joseph Kane. *With:* John Wayne, Ann Dvorak, Joseph Schildkraut. **92 mins.** No rating. Beta, VHS **($39.95).** Republic. ★★

In this western-comedy set in 1906 San Francisco, a

gambler and a rancher clash over a saloon singer. Their problems are resolved when the infamous earthquake hits. This ambitious Republic production is entertaining, but it doesn't have as much action as Wayne's programmers. Watch for *Gone With the Wind*'s Butterfly McQueen.

FLAMING FRONTIERS (1938) B/W. *Dir.:* Ray Taylor and Alan James. *With:* Johnny Mack Brown, Eleanor Hansen, Charles Middleton. **298 mins.** No rating. Beta, VHS **($99.95).** Video Yesteryear. ★★

A 15-episode serial from Universal Studios starring Johnny Mack Brown. The serial format allows for detailed plots, lots of action, and dozens of cliff-hangers, all of which occur here in abundance. Hansen plays the beautiful Mary whose father is threatened by nasty Bart Eaton. Brown wants to help but has his own problems when he is framed for murder and thrown in jail. In the meantime, Indians attack and the town is burned. Even Buffalo Bill joins the action! Seeing the entire 298-minute serial may be too much in one sitting, but limited viewings should be fun.

FLAMING STAR (1960) C. *Dir.:* Don Siegel. *With:* Elvis Presley, Barbara Eden, Dolores Del Rio, Steve Forrest. **101 mins.** No rating. Beta, VHS **($59.98)**; CED **($19.98).** Key. ★★★

Elvis stars as a hot-tempered half-breed caught up in the struggle to keep the peace between the Kiowas and the white settlers. The script is highly sensitive in terms of racial themes, and the performances of all the principals are very powerful. Director Siegel refused Elvis any singing scenes over the protests of the producers and Elvis' manager, Col. Tom Parker. A compromise was reached and Elvis was allowed to sing the title ballad over the credit sequence. It's one of Elvis' best films and was made during a time when the popular singer was serious about his acting career.

FOR A FEW DOLLARS MORE (1967) C. *Dir.:* Sergio Leone. *With:* Clint Eastwood, Lee Van Cleef, Gian Maria Volonte, Mara Krupp, Klaus Kinski. **125 mins.** No rating. Beta, VHS **($59.98)**; Laser **($39.98)**; CED **($29.98).** Key.® ★★½

Based on the Japanese samurai film *Sanjuro,* this follow-up to *A Fistful of Dollars* (see review) is about a pair of rival bounty hunters (Eastwood and Van Cleef) who form a shaky alliance

For a Few Dollars More

Fort Apache

in order to capture a band of bank robbers. Beautifully photographed, it's as violent as its predecessor but demonstrates occasional flashes of humor. For those who enjoyed the original.

FORBIDDEN TRAILS (1941) B/W. *Dir.:* Robert North Bradbury. *With:* Buck Jones, Tim McCoy, Raymond Hatton. **60 mins.** No rating. Beta, VHS **($24.95);** Discount. Beta, VHS **($29.95);** United. ★★★½

Ex-cons try to kill the marshal who sent them up. The best of the "Rough Riders" series, with exciting action and music, and thrills that will please their fans.

FORT APACHE (1948) B/W. *Dir.:* John Ford. *With:* John Wayne, Henry Fonda, Shirley Temple, Victor McLaglen, Pedro Armendariz, John Agar, Ward Bond. **125 mins.** No rating. Beta, VHS **($29.95);** Nostalgia Merchant. Beta, VHS **($34.95);** VidAmerica. ★★★

Ford's first cavalry epic features some of the director's regular players, as well as Temple and her then husband John Agar. Fonda plays a dangerously rigid army officer who doesn't understand the west and doesn't want to. His strictly by-the-book attitude and his unreasonable orders place his troops at the Indians' mercy. A large-scale western with intermittent comic flashes, this is one of Ford's "problem" classics; it never complements the sensitive beauty of its imagery with genuinely sensitive characters, despite excellent performances. (The film is also available in a "John Wayne Gift Pack" with *Flying Leathernecks* and *She Wore A Yellow Ribbon* for $99.00 from VidAmerica.)

FRISCO KID, THE (1979) C. *Dir.:* Robert Aldrich. *With:* Gene Wilder, Harrison Ford, Ramon Bieri, Penny Peyser. **119 mins.** Rated PG. Beta, VHS **($54.95).** Warner. ★★½

Wilder is a Polish rabbi traveling across the Old West to San Francisco and falling in with a friendly bank robber (Ford). Together they encounter thieves, Indians, and crooked townsfolk. A strange premise, but it is lighthearted enough to work. Ford's performance is charming, but Wilder is somewhat overbearing.

FRONTIER HORIZON (1939) B/W. *Dir.:* George Sherman. *With:* John Wayne, Phyllis Isley (Jennifer Jones), Ray Corrigan, Raymond Hatton. **55 mins.** No rating. Beta, VHS **($19.95).** Blackhawk. ★★★

The last of Wayne's "Three Mesquiteers" films; Ray Corrigan and Raymond Hatton complete the trio. In this one, the heroes help homesteaders fight corrupt land speculators who want to flood the settlers' land to create a reservoir. Jennifer Jones in her first movie plays the female lead under her real name, Phyllis Isley. The movie's original title, *The New Frontier,* was changed when an earlier Wayne film with the same name was discovered.

FRONTIER PONY EXPRESS (1939) B/W. *Dir.:* Joseph Kane. *With:* Roy Rogers, Mary Hart (Lynne Roberts), Monte Blue, Noble Johnson, Raymond Hatton. **54 mins.** No rating. Beta, VHS **($N/A).** Nostalgia Merchant. ★½

A small-scale, slow-paced early Rogers outing. The cast provides more interest than the plot. Mary Hart (known as Lynne Roberts in all but her films with Rogers) was one of Rogers' frequent female costars before Dale Evans arrived on the scene. Old-timer Monte Blue, a romantic star of silent films who was part Cherokee Indian, is one of the reliable supporting cast. George Montgomery appears in an early role under his real name, George Letz.

FRONTIERSMAN, THE (1938) B/W. *Dir.:* Lesley Selander. *With:* Hopalong Cassidy (William Boyd), George "Gabby" Hayes,

Russell Hayden, Evelyn Venable, Clara Kimball Young, Roy Barcroft. **74 mins.** No rating. Beta, VHS **($24.95).** Discount. ★★½

An above average but slow-paced Hopalong Cassidy western in which Hoppy helps schoolteacher Evelyn Venable with her boys' school. The St. Brendan's Boys' Choir provides the music, and silent stars William Duncan and Clara Kimball Young join regulars Gabby Hayes and Russell Hayden in the fun. Features the usual dramatic Hoppy climax.

GALLOPING DYNAMITE (1937) B/W. *Dir.:* Harry Fraser. *With:* Kermit Maynard, Ariane Allen, John Merton, David Sharpe, Budd Buster. **58 mins.** No rating. Beta, VHS **($29.95).** Video Dimensions. ★★

A routine Kermit Maynard low-budget oater highlighted by fast riding and good action. Although Maynard starred in his own western series during the silent era, he found it difficult to find work in talking pictures. His older brother, Ken, a popular cowboy star, gave Kermit a job as his double, and Kermit was soon starring in his own low-budget westerns. Nothing special.

GHOST PATROL (1936) B/W. *Dir.:* Sam Newfield. *With:* Tim McCoy, Claudia Dell, Walter Miller, Dick Curtis, Slim Whitaker. **57 mins.** No rating. Beta, VHS **($29.95).** United. ★★½

An offbeat story in which a crooked death-ray inventor starts shooting down mail planes, and G-man Tim McCoy is called in to investigate. One of a series of low-budget McCoy vehicles produced by Puritan Pictures. Old-time villains Walter Miller, Wheeler Oakman, and Dick Curtis are fine in supporting roles, and McCoy is always worth watching. Recommended.

GHOST TOWN GOLD (1936) B/W. *Dir.:* Joseph Kane. *With:* Bob Livingston, Ray Corrigan, Max Terhune, Kay Hughes, Yakima Canutt, Frank Hagney, LeRoy Mason. **55 mins.** No rating. Beta, VHS **($24.95).** Discount. ★★

Another low-budget "Three Mesquiteers" adventure with Livingston, Corrigan, and Terhune as the western trio. This one was the second in the series and emphasized in the screenplay the real competitiveness that existed between Corrigan and Livingston. This was Terhune's first "Mesquiteer" outing and he proved more popular than his predecessor Syd Saylor. However, Terhune, also a ventriloquist, incorporated his dummy into the films, which did not fit the image painted in the novels on which the series was based.

GHOST TOWN LAW (1942) B/W. *Dir.:* Howard Bretherton. *With:* Buck Jones, Tim McCoy, Raymond Hatton. **62 mins.** No rating. Beta, VHS **($24.95).** Discount. ★★½

Mysterious killings and strange goings-on in an old mansion call for an investigation by the Rough Riders. This entertaining film features a good nighttime chase scene and lots of exciting action.

GIANT (1956) C. *Dir.:* George Stevens. *With:* Rock Hudson, Elizabeth Taylor, James Dean, Mercedes McCambridge, Carroll Baker, Chill Wills, Dennis Hopper, Sal Mineo. **201 mins.** Rated G. Beta Hi-Fi, VHS Hi-Fi **($59.95);** Laser **($39.98).** Warner. ®
★★★½

A big-as-all-outdoors film, based on an Edna Ferber novel, that examines two generations of a family of Texas cattle ranchers. Dean turns in an electric performance (his last) as Hudson's rival for Taylor's love, though his scenes as the aging Jett Rink don't ring quite as true. A variety of themes intertwine in the ambitious plot, including racial tension, the cattlemen vs. the oil barons, and Taylor's painful adjustment to the Texas lifestyle. The epic proportions of the story, captured so beautifully on the big screen in CinemaScope, will surely be lost on the small screen.

GOIN' SOUTH (1978) C. *Dir.:* Jack Nicholson. *With:* Jack Nicholson, Mary Steenburgen, Christopher Lloyd, John Belushi. **109 mins.** Rated PG. Beta, VHS **($49.95);** Laser **($29.95).** Paramount. ★★½

An uneven yet charming comedy-western in which Nicholson saves himself from being lynched by marrying a spinster (Steenburgen) who wants him to work in her mine. Both Steenburgen and John Belushi made their film debuts here.

GOLDEN STALLION, THE/KING OF THE COWBOYS (1949/1943) C/B&W. *Dir.:* NA/Joseph Kane. *With:* Roy Rogers, Dale Evans, Estelita Rodriguez, Pat Brady/Roy Rogers, Smiley Burnette, Peggy Moran, Gerald Mohr. **121 mins.** No rating. Beta, VHS **($39.95).** Republic. ★★★½/★★½

Trigger takes center stage in *The Golden Stallion,* a story about wild horses and diamond smugglers. Fans of Roy Rogers should heartily enjoy this somewhat unusual film, which features the Riders of the Purple Sage as Roy's musical backup.

In *King of the Cowboys,* Rogers plays a WWII government agent trying to save American soldiers from a band of ruthless saboteurs. The film marks the start of Rogers' reign as "King of the Cowboys"—the number one moneymaking western star. He succeeded Gene Autry, who left the film business to enlist in the army. (*King of the Cowboys* is also available from Discount for $24.95.)

GOOD, THE BAD, AND THE UGLY, THE (1968) C. *Dir.:* Sergio Leone. *With:* Clint Eastwood, Eli Wallach, Lee Van Cleef. **161 mins.** No rating. Beta, VHS **($79.95);** Laser **($39.98);** CED **($39.98).** CBS/Fox. ★★★

More plot and more humor make this last entry in the violence-filled Leone/Eastwood trilogy (see *A Fistful of Dollars* and *For a Few Dollars More*) also the best. Three outlaws (Eastwood, Van Cleef, and Wallach in, respectively, the title roles) search for a treasure that was lost during the Civil War. The great photography, performances, and score make this unforgettable entertainment.

GREAT K&A TRAIN ROBBERY, THE (1926) B/W. *Dir.:* Lewis Seiler. *With:* Tom Mix, Dorothy Dwan, William Walling, Harry Grippe. **55 mins.** Silent. No rating. Beta, VHS **($N/A).** Glenn Video Vistas. ★★★★

This is a great introduction to the great silent cowboy star Tom Mix. Packed with fast action and marvelous scenery, this film shows the star at his best. Tony the Wonder Horse performs fantastic daredevil stunts. Don't miss it.

GREY FOX, THE (1983) C. *Dir.:* Philip Borsos. *With:* Richard Farnsworth, Jackie Burroughs, Wayne Robson. **92 mins.** Rated PG. Beta, VHS **($69.95).** Media. ★★★

Richard Farnsworth gives a solid performance as a stagecoach bandit who, after serving a 33-year sentence, is released from San Quentin Prison "into the 20th century." With nothing but outdated criminal experience, the aging outlaw doesn't fit in modern society. However, when he sees his first movie, the silent classic *The Great Train Robbery,* he realizes he must adapt and update his methods, and begins a new life—robbing trains. Beautifully photographed on location in northwestern Canada and boasting terrific, low-key performances, the film is highly recommended.

GUNFIGHT AT THE O.K. CORRAL (1957) C. *Dir.:* John Sturges. *With:* Burt Lancaster, Kirk Douglas, Rhonda Fleming, Jo Van Fleet, John Ireland, Lee Van Cleef. **122 mins.** No rating. Beta, VHS **($59.95);** Laser **($29.95);** CED **($19.98).** Paramount. ★★★

Lancaster plays Wyatt Earp and Douglas stars as Doc Holliday in this effective interpretation of the West's most famous gun battle. The film does not dwell on the gunfight, however, but focuses on the bond between Earp and Holliday. Beautiful color photography shot mostly on location in Vista-Vision enhances the well-written script and serious portrayals of the legendary figures. The O.K. Corral showdown is on screen for five minutes, but took 44 hours to film.

GUNMAN FROM BODIE, THE (1941) B/W. *Dir.:* Spencer Bennet. *With:* Buck Jones, Tim McCoy, Raymond Hatton, Christopher McIntyre, David O'Brien. **63 mins.** No rating. Beta, VHS **($24.95).** Discount. ★★★

A marshal finds a baby in its murdered parents' cabin, and vows to bring the killers to justice. One of the best of the "Rough Riders" series, with the trio again donning disguises until the climax.

GUNPLAY (1951) B/W. *Dir.:* Lesley Selander. *With:* Tim Holt, Joan Dixon, Richard Martin. **61 mins.** No rating. Beta, VHS **($N/A).** Nostalgia Merchant. ★★½

A cowboy and his sidekick protect an 11-year-old orphan and help him fight his parent's murderers. A routine Holt entry.

GUN RANGER (1934) B/W. *Dir.:* Robert N. Bradbury. *With:* Bob Steele, Eleanor Stewart, John Merton. **56 mins.** No rating. Beta, VHS **($24.95).** Discount. ★★½

A routine but entirely satisfying Bob Steele western in which the star plays an ex-Texas Ranger who's going after the bad guys. John Merton plays the villain trying to take over Eleanor Stewart's ranch. Popular cowboy star Steele began his career as Bob Bradbury, Jr., acting in silents for his father, a director who specialized in low-budget westerns, of which this is an excellent example.

GUNS OF FURY (1945) B/W. *Dir.:* N/A. *With:* Duncan Renaldo. **60 mins.** No rating. Beta, VHS **($47.95).** United. ★★

Renaldo stars as the Cisco Kid in this B-western released through Monogram Studios. Renaldo was the third actor to play the Kid in films, and became the most popular, later reviving his role for a successful television series. The two previous actors who appeared as the Kid played him as a vicious outlaw, but Renaldo refused to present him as the stereotyped Mexican killer-bandit, and instead played him as a dashing Latin hero.

HANG 'EM HIGH (1967) C. *Dir.:* Ted Post. *With:* Clint Eastwood, Inger Stevens, Ed Begley, Pat Hingle. **114 mins.** No rating. Beta, VHS **($59.98);** Laser **($34.98);** CED **($19.98).** CBS/Fox. ★★½

Clint Eastwood manages to survive his own hanging, and then seeks revenge against the men who strung him up. Post (who had directed several episodes of Eastwood's *Rawhide* television series) attempted to duplicate the style of the spaghetti westerns of Sergio Leone, but failed to capture their sarcastic wit or epic scope. There is, however, much action and good performances by well-seasoned western character actors.

The Grey Fox

Hang 'em High

HAUNTED RANCH (1943) B/W. *Dir.:* Robert Tansey. *With:* John King, David Sharpe, Max Terhune, Rex Lease, Budd Buster. **57 mins.** No rating. Beta, VHS **($19.98).** Blackhawk. ★★

A mystery-western featuring a trio of cowboys known as the Range Busters. Here they search for the location of a secret hidden treasure. Clues to the location are to be found in the words of an old cowboy song. Terhune had previously been in the "Three Mesquiteers" western series, and Sharpe was a well-known stunt man.

HEARTLAND (1981) C. *Dir.:* Richard Pearce. *With:* Rip Torn, Conchata Ferrell, Barry Primus, Lilia Skala, Megan Folson. **95 mins.** Rated PG. Beta, VHS **($69.95).** Thorn EMI/HBO. ★★★★

An understated, beautifully photographed film. In the early 1900s, a penniless widow (Ferrell) arrives in the Dakota territory with her young daughter to work as a housekeeper for Torn, an unmarried, middle-aged rancher who is set in his ways. Together, they battle the hardships of life in the frontier wilderness. A moving film with wonderful performances. Don't miss this one.

HEART OF THE GOLDEN WEST (1942) B/W. *Dir.:* Joseph Kane. *With:* Roy Rogers, Smiley Burnette, George "Gabby" Hayes, Walter Catlett, Paul Harvey. **54 mins.** No rating. Beta, VHS **($39.95).** Video Yesteryear. ★★★

This is Rogers' first big-budget musical, filmed after Gene Autry left the studio to enlist in the army. The plot centers around a group of cattlemen who get angry when they are cheated by Paul Harvey, the owner of a trucking company who is charging too much to transport the herds. Roy saves the day when he convinces captain Walter Catlett to let the ranchers ship their cattle aboard his steamboat. This is a funnier than usual Rogers picture because it features not one but two comic sidekicks, Smiley Burnette and Gabby Hayes.

HEART OF THE RIO GRANDE (1942) B/W. *Dir.:* William Morgan. *With:* Gene Autry, Smiley Burnette, Fay McKenzie, Edith Fellows, Joseph Strauch, Jr. **70 mins.** No rating. Beta, VHS **($34.98).** Blackhawk. ★★½

A spoiled young schoolgirl is forced to accompany her classmates on a trip to a dude ranch. Once there, she sends her busy, wealthy father falsified photographs of the supposed rough treatment she is getting at the ranch. Her father rushes to her rescue, only to find out what she has done. Ultimately he realizes that he is not paying enough attention to his daughter. A highly amusing and piquant B-western, set in contemporary times, with a more novel plot than usual. A good film for the entire family.

HEART OF THE ROCKIES (1937) B/W. *Dir.:* Joseph Kane. *With:* Bob Livingston, Ray Corrigan, Max Terhune. **54 mins.** No rating. Beta, VHS **($N/A).** Nostalgia Merchant. ★★★

One of the best of the early "Three Mesquiteers" westerns with Bob Livingston, Ray Corrigan, and Max Terhune. Bear killers, child brides, and a vicious fistfight between Livingston and Yakima Canutt are some of the highlights of this unusual production.

HEAVEN'S GATE (1980) C. *Dir.:* Michael Cimino. *With:* Kris Kristofferson, Christopher Walken, John Hurt, Isabelle Huppert, Jeff Bridges, Joseph Cotten. **219 mins.** Rated R. Beta, VHS **($69.95)**. MGM/UA. ★★½

When the full-length, 219-minute version of *Heaven's Gate* opened in November of 1980, it was declared by the critics to be an unqualified disaster. This $38-million film is based on a historical incident involving an 1890s range war in Wyoming between cattle barons and the immigrants who were encroaching on the range. The relationships between the characters are never clearly defined, and many of the scenes seem strung together haphazardly. The film is worth viewing, however, for the stunning beauty of its cinematography. Sometimes a glorious fiasco is more interesting viewing than an average Hollywood feature, which is the case here.

HELDORADO (1946) B/W. *Dir.:* William Witney. *With:* Roy Rogers, Dale Evans, Bob Nolan and the Sons of the Pioneers, Paul Harvey, Rex Lease, Clayton Moore. **54 mins.** No rating. Beta, VHS **($24.95)**. Discount. ★★

Nevada's "Frontier Days" celebration is the background for this mild-mannered Roy Rogers film. In addition to Dale Evans, cowboy stars Clayton Moore (the Lone Ranger) and Rex Lease head up the supporting cast. This film was released in the same year as the superior *My Pal Trigger (see review),* and suffers in comparison. *HELDORADO* is available on a double bill with *EYES OF TEXAS* from Nostalgia Merchant.

HEROES OF THE HILLS (1938) B/W. *Dir.:* George Sherman. *With:* Bob Livingston, Ray Corrigan, Max Terhune, Priscilla Lawso. **54 mins.** No rating. Beta, VHS **($N/A).** Nostalgia Merchant. ★★½

One of the better entries in the "Three Mesquiteers" series, which is not saying much. This very low-budget vehicle features Livingston, Corrigan, and Terhune as the happy-go-lucky trio, and Lawso, formerly of the "Flash Gordon" films, as the female love interest. Here the boys offer the ranch as a prison farm in the interest of penal reform. The series as a whole is only for die-hard B-western fans.

HIDDEN GOLD (1933) B/W. *Dir.:* Arthur Rosson. *With:* Tom Mix, Judith Barrie, Raymond Hatton, Eddie Gribbon, Roy Moore. **57 mins.** No rating. Beta, VHS **($N/A).** Video Connection. ★★½

Mix, in one of his few talkies, tries to infiltrate a group of outlaws in order to find stolen money. The film is not one of his best, perhaps because while filming an action sequence on location, Tony the Wonder Horse stepped in a gopher hole, injuring both himself and Mix. Tony was then retired to Mix's ranch at Mixville and replaced by Tony, Jr. Mix, then over 50 years old, recovered quickly and went on to make several more features.

HIGH NOON (1952) B/W. *Dir.:* Fred Zinnemann. *With:* Gary Cooper, Grace Kelly, Lloyd Bridges, Thomas Mitchell, Katy Jurado. **84 mins.** No rating. Beta, VHS **($59.95);** CED **($19.98).** Republic. ★★★½

A just-married sheriff is ready to retire when he learns that one of the men he put in prison is coming back to town with his brothers—bent on revenge. The cowardly townspeople refuse to help and his Quaker bride wants him to leave town peacefully, but the marshal stays to face the bad guys alone. A lean and polished western, with a haunting musical score and brilliant cross-cut editing that heightens the dramatic showdown. Cooper won a well-deserved Oscar for his portrayal of the steely-eyed lawman.

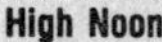
High Noon

High Plains Drifter

HIGH PLAINS DRIFTER (1973) C. *Dir.:* Clint Eastwood. *With:* Clint Eastwood, Verna Bloom, Marianna Hill, Mitchell Ryan. **105 mins.** Rated R. Beta, VHS **($69.95).** MCA. ★★★

A brooding, almost mystical western starring Eastwood as a stranger who arrives in the frontier town of Largo. He is enlisted by the citizens to defend the town against a group of men, recently released from jail, who have sworn revenge against the townsfolk. After the stranger demands that all of Largo's buildings be painted red and that the town sign on the outskirts of Largo be changed to "Hell," the corrupt town officials fear his mysterious ways but fail in an attempt to kill him. The film, shot in the style of spaghetti westerns, represents Eastwood's first directorial effort, and was criticized for being too symbolic (low-angle shots, heavy-handed score, deliberate cross-cutting). *High Plains Drifter* resembles in plot and style Eastwood's 1985 *Pale Rider* (see review).

HILLS OF UTAH, THE (1951) B/W. *Dir.:* John English. *With:* Gene Autry, Pat Buttram, Denver Pyle, Elaine Riley, Donna Martell. **70 mins.** No rating. Beta, VHS **($34.98).** Blackhawk. ★★½

As a feud rages between a mine operator and the local cattlemen, Gene returns to his hometown to find his father's murderer. Within all the turmoil, Gene, also a doctor, tries to establish a hospital. Veteran character actor Pyle makes an early appearance and Buttram plays the comic sidekick.

HIS FIGHTING BLOOD (1935) B/W. *Dir.:* John English. *With:* Kermit Maynard, Polly Ann Young, Ted Adams, Paul Fix, Joseph Girard, Frank O'Connor. **63 mins.** No rating. Beta, VHS **($29.95).** Video Dimensions. ★★

A Canadian mountie goes undercover to search for some stolen money. Based on a James Oliver Curwood story, this film has some okay action and music, but is basically only a routine entry in Kermit Maynard's mountie series. Polly Ann Young (Loretta's sister) provides the love interest.

HIT THE SADDLE (1937) B/W. *Dir.:* Mack Wright. *With:* Bob Livingston, Ray Corrigan, Max Terhune, Rita Casino (Hayworth). **54 mins.** No rating. Beta, VHS **($N/A).** Video Connection. ★★

An early entry in the "Three Mesquiteers" series, with a stronger plot line than most of the later vehicles will have. Here the trio help in the roundup of a herd of wild horses. The roundup is hampered when one of the boys (Livingston) becomes infatuated with the beautiful Rita Casino (later Rita Hayworth). The romance temporarily breaks up the trio—until the action-packed climax reunites the three men. Footage of the stallion fight from the silent film *The Devil Horse* was incorporated to enhance the action.

HOMBRE (1967) C. *Dir.:* Martin Ritt. *With:* Paul Newman, Fredric March, Richard Boone, Diane Cilento, Cameron Mitchell, Barbara Rush, Martin Balsam. **111 mins.** No rating. Beta, VHS **($59.95).** CBS/Fox. ★★★

Paul Newman stars as a white man raised by Apaches as an Indian. When the stagecoach he is traveling on is attacked by bandits trying to steal money that corrupt Indian agent March has embezzled, Newman must defend his white, helpless fellow passengers. Interesting characters, good performances, and some real suspense make this an exciting drama.

HOME IN OKLAHOMA (1947) B/W. *Dir.:* William Witney. *With:* Roy Rogers, Dale Evans, George "Gabby" Hayes, Carol Hughes. **54 mins.** No rating. Beta, VHS **($24.95).** Discount. ★★★

Roy Rogers and frequent costar Dale Evans got hitched the year this film was made. It's a routine but enjoyable movie with amusing comic high jinks from Gabby Hayes and musical support from the Sons of the Pioneers. There's also plenty of action as Roy tracks down a killer.

HOPPY SERVES A WRIT (1943) B/W. *Dir.:* George Archainbaud. *With:* Hopalong Cassidy (William Boyd), Andy Clyde, Jay Kirby, Victor Jory, George Reeves, Robert Mitchum, Roy Barcroft. **67 mins.** No rating. Beta, VHS **($25.00).** Cumberland. ★★★½

Clarence E. Mulford, creator of the Hopalong Cassidy character, wrote his last Hoppy novel in 1941. It was called *Hopalong Cassidy Serves a Writ* and serves as the basis for this, one of the best in the popular, long-running western series. The fast-moving plot has Hoppy chasing an outlaw gang across the state line. Andy Clyde is an appropriate comic foil, but Jay Kirby is colorless and boring in his role. Robert Mitchum has a small role as a bad guy. He got the role when the actor who was originally cast was thrown from his horse and injured. Also watch for George (Superman) Reeves in a bit part.

HOPPY'S HOLIDAY (1947) B/W. *Prod.:* William Boyd. *With:* Hopalong Cassidy (William Boyd), Rand Brooks, Andy Clyde. **59 mins.** No rating. Beta, VHS **($59.95).** Blackhawk. ★★½

Hopalong's vacation is cut short when the local bank is robbed in a mysterious manner. One of the later films in the Hopalong Cassidy series, with the usual humorous antics.

HORSE SOLDIERS, THE (1959) C. *Dir.:* John Ford. *With:* John Wayne, William Holden, Constance Towers. **119 mins.** No rating. Beta, VHS **($59.98);** CED **($19.98).** CBS/Fox. 🗨® ★★½

Wayne and Holden each received record salaries of $750,000 for this big-budget epic based on an actual Civil War mission. Wayne plays a tough Union colonel ordered to sabotage Confederate communication and transport lines by destroying the railroad center at Newport Station, Mississippi. Wayne and his troops must battle through more than 300 miles of enemy territory, facing grievous injuries and casualties. The peace-loving doctor (Holden) accompanying the raiding party is forced to clean up the bloody messes left after the skirmishes. He hates Wayne for driving the men to their deaths, and Wayne hates doctors because his wife died in an unnecessary operation. Overlong and with dull stretches, this is a lesser film from the great director John Ford, and is recommended only to hard-core Ford or Wayne buffs. The widely publicized appearance by veteran cowboy star Hoot Gibson is in reality only a flash on the screen.

HUD (1963) B/W. *Dir.:* Martin Ritt. *With:* Paul Newman, Patricia Neal, Melvyn Douglas, Brandon de Wilde. **112 mins.** No rating. Beta, VHS **($66.95)**; Laser **($29.95)**; CED **($19.98).** Paramount. ★★★★

A powerful contemporary western about alienation and the decay of society. Newman stars as Hud, the ruthless, selfish son of a moralistic, unforgiving Texas cattle rancher (Douglas). De Wilde plays the youth who idolizes his Uncle Hud, and loves but is afraid of his grandfather. Neal plays their housekeeper, a woman who desires Hud but knows that he's no good. The stars all turn in excellent performances; Neal and Douglas won Academy Awards for, respectively, Best Actress and Best Supporting Actor. The dry, dusty Texas ranch provides an appropriately bleak backdrop for the embittered cynicism of the characters and the emotional tension between them. Superbly written and directed.

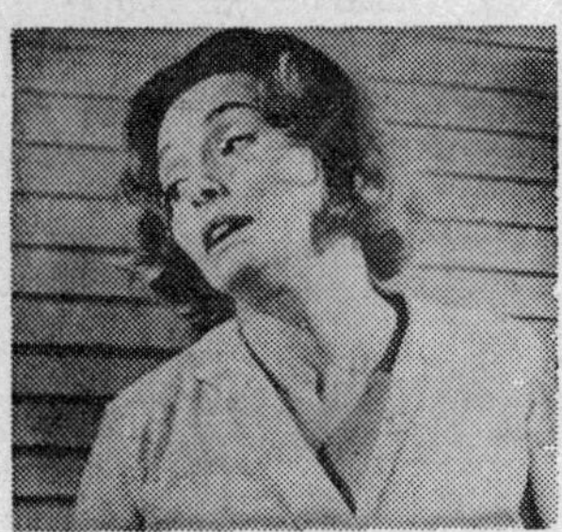

Hud

In Old California

IN OLD CALIFORNIA (1942) B/W. *Dir.:* William McGann. *With:* John Wayne, Binnie Barnes, Albert Dekker, Patsy Kelly, Helen Parrish, Edgar Kennedy. **89 mins.** No rating. Beta, VHS **($39.95).** Republic. ★★

During the days of the California gold rush, pharmacist Wayne moves from sedate Boston to rough, wild Sacramento. There, he has a run-in with the crooked town boss (Dekker). A predictable, old-fashioned, but entertaining John Wayne vehicle.

IN OLD NEW MEXICO (1945) B/W. *Dir.:* Phil Rosen. *With:* Duncan Renaldo, Martin Garralaga, Gwen Kenyon, Pedro de Cordoba. **60 mins.** No rating. Beta, VHS **($39.95).** Video Yesteryear. ★★

Duncan Renaldo had already established a following with his appearances as one of the popular "Three Mesquiteers" when Monogram starred him as the Cisco Kid. In this, his second film in the role, he kidnaps a beautiful senorita to save her from a fate worse than death. The previous Cisco pictures, which were from Fox Studios, boasted higher production values and more elaborate costumes and sets, but Monogram introduced to the series the comic character Pancho (based on *Don Quixote's* Sancho Panza). Martin Garralaga, a former opera singer, was the first to costar as Cisco's partner, adding a welcome, humanizing touch to the films. Ironically, Garralaga was allergic to horses and had a difficult time filming the westerns. An enjoyable film from an enjoyable series.

IN OLD OKLAHOMA. See WAR OF THE WILDCATS.

IN OLD SANTA FE (1934) B/W. *Dir.:* David Howard. *With:* Ken Maynard, Evalyn Knapp, Gene Autry, Smiley Burnette, George "Gabby" Hayes, H. B. Warner. **64 mins.** No rating. Beta, VHS **($24.95).** Discount. ★★★

Ken Maynard is framed for murder after losing his horse, Tarzan, in a crooked race in this superior independent western. Although it features splendid action and a fine cast, the film is famous today only as Gene Autry's film debut. Autry plays himself, sings a few songs, and steals the film from star Maynard. A must for B-western buffs.

JEREMIAH JOHNSON (1972) C. *Dir.:* Sydney Pollack. *With:* Robert Redford, Will Geer, Stephan Gierasch. **108 mins.** Rated PG. Beta, VHS **($39.98);** CED **($19.98).** Warner. ★★★

The title character is a strong, silent type who, in the 1830s, gives up civilization to lead the harsh life of a mountain man. He almost starves to death his first year, but an old, experienced trapper (Geer) rescues him and teaches him the basics of life in the Rockies. Johnson later takes in a homeless boy and marries an Indian woman. When his family is murdered by Crow Indians in retaliation for an unintentional offense, Johnson vows revenge. Robert Redford does a good job with this atypical role, but the movie is sometimes ponderous and slow. It's worth seeing, however, just for its breathtaking photography and scenery.

JESSE JAMES AT BAY (1941) B/W. *Dir.:* Joseph Kane. *With:* Roy Rogers, George "Gabby" Hayes, Gale Storm, Sally Payne, Roy Barcroft, Rex Lease. **54 mins.** No rating. Beta, VHS **($24.95).** Discount. ★★

This minor Rogers western features some offbeat casting—Roy appears in a dual role. He plays both Jesse James and a gambler hired to impersonate the famous outlaw in a fight against the railroad. It's an interesting premise, but the movie is sluggish and doesn't overcome its low-budget quickie origins. It wasn't until 1942, when Gene Autry left Republic for the army, that the studio began giving Rogers' pictures bigger budgets and more publicity.

JOE KIDD (1972) C. *Dir.:* John Sturges. *With:* Clint Eastwood, Robert Duvall, John Saxon, Don Stroud. **88 mins.** Rated PG. Beta, VHS **($69.95).** MCA. ★★½

It's the Mexican-Americans against the land barons of New Mexico in this fairly pedestrian Clint Eastwood outing. Eastwood plays a bounty hunter hired by wealthy tycoon Duvall to track down and kill the leader (Saxon) of a gang of Mexican bandits. Eastwood eventually takes the side of the Mexicans, and the final confrontation is appropriately brutal.

Johnny Guitar

JOHNNY GUITAR (1953) C. *Dir.:* Nicholas Ray. *With:* Joan Crawford, Sterling Hayden, Scott Brady, Mercedes McCambridge. **110 mins.** No rating. Beta, VHS **($39.95).** Republic. ★★★★

This uncanny, psychological western features Crawford as a gambling hall proprietress who clashes with morality-monger McCambridge, while falling in love with a sharpshooter (Hayden) who has traded in his guns for a guitar. The movie's rich use of Freudian symbolism won the applause of European directors (Francois Truffaut said it wasn't "about horses," while Bernardo Bertolucci dubbed it "the first of the Baroque westerns"), and gay audiences championed its reversal of sexual stereotypes. Above all, it's a western at its best—exciting, passionate, and inspired. Especially recommended to viewers who can't stand westerns.

JUNIOR BONNER (1972) C. *Dir.:* Sam Peckinpah. *With:* Steve McQueen, Robert Preston, Ida Lupino, Ben Johnson, Joe Don Baker. **103 mins.** Rated PG. Beta, VHS **($59.98);** CED **($19.98).** CBS/Fox. ★★★

McQueen delivers a bravura performance as Junior Bonner, an aging rodeo star who returns to his Arizona hometown to ride in a local rodeo and finds that everything has changed. His father drinks; his parents are separated; and his brother has cut up the family ranch and sold it off in little pieces. The Old West is dying, and all that men like Bonner and his father have left are their dreams and their outdated, fading skills. An unusually restrained effort from director Peckinpah, this is a quiet, unassuming film, marked by good acting (especially from Lupino and Preston as Bonner's parents) and some nice comic touches.

KANSAN, THE (1943) B/W. *Dir.:* George Archainbaud. *With:* Richard Dix, Jane Wyatt, Victor Jory, Albert Dekker, Roy Rogers. **79 mins.** No rating. Beta, VHS **($19.95).** Kartes. ★★★

A strong-willed marshal battles outlaws and corrupt officials to bring peace to the town of Broken Lance. This fast-moving action-western is well paced and well acted. Dix turns in an effective performance, and Jane Wyatt is as lovely as always.

KENTUCKIAN, THE (1955) C. *Dir.:* Burt Lancaster. *With:* Burt Lancaster, Diana Lynn, Walter Matthau, John McIntire, John Carradine. **104 mins.** No rating. Beta, VHS **($59.98);** CED **($19.98).** CBS/Fox. ★★

A Kentucky frontiersman and his son try to build a new life in 1820s Texas. The slow-moving story is highlighted by an exciting bullwhip fight and some refined comic touches. Walter Matthau made his film debut here, and Diana Lynn turns in a strong supporting performance.

KING OF THE BULLWHIP (1951) B/W. *Dir.:* Ron Ormond. *With:* Lash LaRue, Al "Fuzzy" St. John, Jack Holt, Tom Neal, Anne Gwynne, Dennis Moore. **59 mins.** No rating. Beta, VHS **($24.98).** Discount. ★

A later LaRue B-western featuring Buster Crabbe's sidekick, Fuzzy St. John, in the comic supporting role. Most of LaRue's films were considered substandard in comparison to other B-westerns, but this one is even worse. Don't waste your time.

KING OF THE COWBOYS. See THE GOLDEN STALLION/KING OF THE COWBOYS.

KIT CARSON (1940) B/W. *Dir.:* George B. Seitz. *With:* Jon Hall, Lynn Bari, Dana Andrews, Ward Bond. **97 mins.** No rating. Beta, VHS **($N/A).** Nostalgia Merchant. ★★½

The famous frontiersman Christopher "Kit" Carson (Hall) guides a wagon train safely to California despite the interference of the cavalry officer leading the expedition (Andrews). On the way, Hall and Andrews fight hostile Indians and compete for the love of beautiful Lynn Bari. A routine but entertaining film with lots of action. Watch for Clayton (*The Lone Ranger*) Moore.

LADY TAKES A CHANCE, A (1943) B/W. *Dir.:* William A. Seiter. *With:* John Wayne, Jean Arthur, Phil Silvers, Charles Winninger, Hans Conried, Grady Sutton. **86 mins.** No rating. Beta, VHS **($39.95).** VidAmerica. ★★½

More of a light comedy than an action-filled western, this film is worth seeing for the unique pairing of John Wayne and Jean Arthur. He plays a rodeo cowboy, and she's the vacationing New York secretary who falls in love with him. Amusing.

LAND OF THE LAWLESS (1947) B/W. *Dir.:* Lambert Hillyer. *With:* Johnny Mack Brown, Raymond Hatton, Christine McIntyre, Tris Coffin, June Harrison. **54 mins.** No rating. Beta, VHS **($24.95).** Discount. ★★½

An above-average B-western from Brown, made for Monogram Pictures at the height of his popularity. Brown's various series generally had better budgets, production values, and directors than other B-westerns, and are usually more enjoyable viewing for that reason. Raymond Hatton from the "Rough Riders" series provides good support.

LAST COMMAND, THE (1955) C. *Dir.:* Frank Lloyd. *With:* Sterling Hayden, Anna Maria Alberghetti, Arthur Hunnicutt, J. Carrol Naish, Richard Carlson, Slim Pickens. **110 mins.** No rating. Beta, VHS **($39.95).** Republic. ★★

The Battle of the Alamo, Republic style. Sterling Hayden stars as Jim Bowie, a Mexican citizen born in Texas whose loyalties are divided when the two territories war over border disputes. He must decide whether to ally himself with Mexican general Santa Anna (Naish) or with Davy Crockett (Hunnicutt) and other frontiersmen defending the Alamo. This is one of Republic's biggest productions, featuring on-location photography; a sumptuous score by Max Steiner; fast, hard action; and an exciting climactic battle. Unfortunately, the movie is burdened with a plodding script and strange casting.

LAST GUN, THE (1964) C. *Dir.:* Serge Bergon. *With:* Cameron Mitchell. **98 mins.** No rating. Beta, VHS **($59.95).** Sagebrush. ★★

Veteran western actor Mitchell stars as Jim Hart, an ex-gunslinger who is forced to take down his guns again to protect his peaceful town from corruption. The film suffers from a too typical plot, and Mitchell is the only recognizable face in the cast.

LAST MUSKETEER, THE (1952) B/W. *Dir.:* William Witney. *With:* Rex Allen, Mary Ellen Kay, Slim Pickens, James Anderson. **67 mins.** No rating. Beta, VHS **($N/A).** Nostalgia Merchant. ★★★★

Rex Allen was one of the last of the singing cowboys, in part because low-budget, independent studios like Republic who specialized in western-musicals were finding them exorbitantly expensive to produce, and television was encroaching on the popularity of such films. But while they lasted, Rex Allen's movies offered fine action. This is one of his best, packed with exciting stunts, fast action, and tuneful melodies.

LAST OF THE PONY RIDERS (1953) B/W. *Dir.:* George Archainbaud. *With:* Gene Autry, Smiley Burnette, Kathleen Case, Dick Jones. **59 mins.** No rating. Beta, VHS **($34.98).** Blackhawk. ★★½

In his last feature film for Columbia, Gene Autry plays an ex-Pony Express rider who is trying to launch a stagecoach line but runs into problems with the bad guys. The movie is well up to Autry's usual high standards and features the songs "Sing Me a Song of the Saddle" and "Sugar Babe." Old crony Smiley Burnette adds to the fun by reuniting with Gene and Champion for their farewell to the big screen.

LAST OUTLAW, THE (1936) B/W. *Dir.:* Christy Cabanne. *With:* Harry Carey, Hoot Gibson, Henry B. Walthall, Tom Tyler, Margaret Callahan. **79 mins.** No rating. Beta, VHS **($N/A).** Video Connection. ★★★

A good, unusual western based on a story by John Ford, who directed a shorter, silent version in 1919. During filming, star Harry Carey acquired the rights to the movie and with Ford planned to film a big-budget remake when World War II ended. Unfortunately, Carey died before the third production could begin. In this entertaining version, Carey plays an old-time outlaw who returns from 20 years in jail to find the west changed and his daughter (Callahan) the mistress of a big-city racketeer (Tyler). He teams up with old pal Hoot Gibson and confronts this New West, using old-fashioned methods to round up Tyler and his gang. Singing cowboy Fred Scott appears in a movie within the movie.

LAST TRAIN FROM GUN HILL (1958) C. *Dir.:* John Sturges. *With:* Kirk Douglas, Anthony Quinn, Carolyn Jones, Earl Holliman. **94 mins.** No rating. Beta, VHS **($59.98).** CBS/Fox. ★★

A tough sheriff (Douglas) has to fight his way out of a lawless town to take his powerful friend's (Quinn) son (Holliman) to trial for raping and murdering the lawman's wife. A well-made drama with competent performances, but the familiar story is not as exciting as it could be. From the same crew that made *Gunfight at the O.K. Corral* (see review).

LAW AND LAWLESS (1932) B/W. *Dir.:* Larry Darmour. *With:* Jack Hoxie, Hilda Moore, Wally Wales, Yakima Canutt, Julian

Rivero, Dixie Starr. **59 mins.** No rating. Beta, VHS **($24.95).** Discount. ★

One of Hoxie's few sound films, which were made for B-studio producers Max and Arthur Alexander. The Alexanders had originally wanted Ken Maynard, but settled for Hoxie (a real-life cowboy and rodeo performer) when Maynard signed with big-time Universal. The peak of Hoxie's popularity occurred in the silent era, and these run-of-the-mill films did nothing to revive his career. Worse-than-usual acting and routine action further mar an already mediocre film.

LAW AND THE OUTLAW, THE (1913) B/W. *Dir.:* N/A. *With:* Tom Mix, Myrtle Stedman. **76 mins.** Silent. No rating. Beta, VHS **($24.98).** Blackhawk. ★★½

Tom Mix stars as Dakota Joe, a fugitive from the law, in this vintage silent western. Joe hires on as a ranch hand in order to lay low for a while, and falls in love with the rancher's pretty daughter. His happiness proves temporary, however, when the sheriff recognizes him. A rare opportunity to see a great western star at his best as well as a fine example of the silent cinema.

LAWLESS FRONTIER (1935) B/W. *Dir.:* Robert N. Bradbury. *With:* John Wayne, George "Gabby" Hayes, Sheila Terry, Yakima Canutt, Buffalo Bill, Jr. **53 mins.** No rating. Beta, VHS **($19.95).** Sony. ★★½

A cowboy (Wayne) returns to his hometown to find the man who killed his parents, and discovers the villain is the sheriff of the town. Before he can do anything, the innocent cowboy is framed for various crimes and must team up with an old gold miner and his pretty granddaughter to capture the real culprits and clear himself of the false accusations. A good Monogram production featuring strong performances. (Sony's tapes are available in Beta Hi-Fi and VHS Hi-Fi.)

LAW OF THE GOLDEN WEST (1949) B/W. *Dir.:* Philip Ford. *With:* Monte Hale, Paul Hurst, Gail Davis, Roy Barcroft, Scott Elliott, Lane Bradford, John Hamilton. **60 mins.** No rating. Beta, VHS **($29.95).** Discount. ★★

Gail Davis makes a spirited leading lady in this otherwise routine Monte Hale western from Republic. Although Hale had an agreeable personality and was backed by Republic's compe

Law of the Golden West

Lightning Raiders

tent crew, his films were only minor efforts at best. This one incorporates footage from better-known films and provides pleasant but lightweight entertainment.

LAWLESS RANGE (1935) B/W. *Dir.:* Robert N. Bradbury. *With:* John Wayne, Sheila Mannors, Yakima Canutt, Jack Curtis, Frank McGlynn, Jr., Glenn Strange. **56 mins.** No rating. Beta, VHS **($19.95).** Spotlite. ★★★

Undercover agent John Wayne is sent to solve the mystery behind a series of unexplained raids on peaceful valley ranchers. During his investigation, Wayne is captured by the gang of bandits, who are led by a greedy banker, putting the ranchers in peril unless he can escape. One of the best of Wayne's early B-westerns for Republic.

LAW OF THE LASH (1947) B/W. *Dir.:* Ray Taylor. *With:* Lash LaRue, Al "Fuzzy" St. John, Mary Scott, Lee Roberts, Jack O'Shea, John Elliott. **54 mins.** No rating. Beta, VHS **($24.95).** Discount. ★

Routine and forgettable. This is another infinitesimal-budget entry in the Lash LaRue series from PRC. Al "Fuzzy" St. John as LaRue's comic sidekick supplies the pratfalls and the film's only entertaining moments.

LAW WEST OF TOMBSTONE, THE (1938) B/W. *Dir.:* Glenn Tryon. *With:* Harry Carey, Tim Holt, Evelyn Brent, Ward Bond,

Kermit Maynard. **73 mins.** No rating. Beta, VHS **($N/A).** Nostalgia Merchant. ★★

A con man (Harry Carey) with a phony gold mine has some trouble with the law. He reforms and takes on the task of cleaning up a wild frontier town. Part of his job includes capturing the dangerous Tonto Kid (Tim Holt in his first role). The film sometimes moves slowly, but is for the most part an entertaining comedy-western. Silent star Evelyn Brent is good as Carey's ex-wife, and future Republic western star Allan "Rocky" Lane has a bit role.

LIFE AND TIMES OF JUDGE ROY BEAN, THE (1972) C. *Dir.:* John Huston. *With:* Paul Newman, Anthony Perkins, Ava Gardner, Victoria Principal, Stacy Keach, Jacqueline Bisset, John Huston, Roddy McDowall, Tab Hunter, Ned Beatty. **123 mins.** Rated PG. Beta, VHS **($59.95).** Warner. ★★½

This revisionist, historically inaccurate western cynically follows the career of Roy Bean (Paul Newman), a self-styled judge with an obsession for actress-beauty Lillie Langtry (Ava Gardner). The script has a tendency to drag, but the judge's encounters with the bizarre characters that wander through his jurisdiction give the movie its zip. Anti-heroic and often brutal, it's a far cry from *The Westerner* (see review), the classic, glossy Hollywood view of the man known as the "law west of the Pecos." This movie may not appeal to traditional western fans, but others will find its black humor engaging.

LIGHTNING RAIDERS (1946) B/W. *Dir.:* Sam Newfield. *With:* Buster Crabbe, Al "Fuzzy" St. John, Mady Lawrence, Ray Brent, Steve Darrell, I. Stanford Jolley. **61 mins.** No rating. Beta, VHS **($29.95).** Discount. ★½

A grade-Z western from PRC Pictures. As usual, production values are practically nonexistent. Buster Crabbe and Al "Fuzzy" St. John head the reliable cast, but even these western stalwarts can't help the film.

LIGHT OF THE WESTERN STARS, THE (1940) B/W. *Dir.:* Lesley Selander. *With:* Victor Jory, Jo Ann Sayers, Russell Hayden, Tom Tyler, Eddie Dean, Noah Beery, Jr., Alan Ladd. **65 mins.** No rating. Beta, VHS **($24.95).** Discount. ★½

This is a minor, slow-moving western, the third version of Zane Grey's famous story of the same title. Both the 1925 silent and the 1930 remake are better. In this one, eastern lady Sayers comes west to reform her outlaw brother (Jory), and falls in love with a drunken cowhand (Hayden). The familiar plot is offset by the offbeat cast. Jory, who usually played villains, appears in a rare sympathetic role; Hayden, most famous as Hopalong Cassidy's sidekick, Lucky, plays the romantic lead (Harry "Pop" Sherman produced both this film and the Hopalong series); and rising star Alan Ladd has a supporting role. Still, there's not enough action to keep the movie interesting.

The Light of the Western Stars

Lights of Old Santa Fe

LIGHTS OF OLD SANTA FE (1947) B/W. *Dir.:* Frank McDonald. *With:* Roy Rogers, Dale Evans, George "Gabby" Hayes, Bob Nolan and the Sons of the Pioneers, Roy Barcroft. **60 mins.** No rating. Beta, VHS **($24.95).** Discount. ★★★

Hero Roy Rogers comes to the aid of a rodeo owner who needs help defending himself against a gang of ruthless crooks. It's one of Roy's better efforts, but unfortunately, most of the videotape versions of this film are missing essential footage; the film originally ran 76 minutes. Featured among the supporting players is Richard Powers, who began acting under his real name, George Duryea; progressed to western star status as Tom Keene in the 1930s; and finished his career with the name Powers, playing mostly character roles.

LITTLE BIG MAN (1970) C. *Dir.:* Arthur Penn. *With:* Dustin Hoffman, Faye Dunaway, Martin Balsam, Chief Dan George,

Jeff Corey, Richard Mulligan. **150 mins.** Rated PG. Beta, VHS **($59.98);** CED **($39.98).** Key. ®★★★

A stinging indictment of the way the U.S. dealt with the American Indians, this movie is sometimes slow and confusing, but is more often ironic and hilarious. It swings from slapstick to arty self-consciousness to vivid, poetic evocation of the west. Dustin Hoffman plays a 121-year-old ex-Indian-fighter who, as the sole white survivor of the battle of Little Bighorn, tells the story of his life to a skeptical contemporary historian. Besides riding with Custer at Little Bighorn, his adventures include being raised by Indians, meeting with western archetypes ranging from a patent-medicine manufacturer to Wild Bill Hickok, and marrying both a Swedish immigrant and an Indian maiden. Hoffman's performance is strong, but Chief Dan George steals the show. Wild, exaggerated, and satiric, this is a highly individual, one-of-a-kind film.

LONE AVENGER, THE (1933) B/W. *Dir.:* Alan James. *With:* Ken Maynard, Muriel Gordon, Jack Rockwell, Charles King, Alan Bridge. **60 mins.** No rating. Beta, VHS **($24.95).** Discount. ★★½

An early Ken Maynard talkie in which the star is framed for a murder he didn't commit. Al Bridge plays the real killer, and he does an effective job conveying the murderer's psychological deterioration as he spends a tension-filled rainstorm waiting for Maynard to find him. The plot is familiar, having already been used in *The Fighting Legion* (1931), which also starred Maynard. But the acting is adequate and the atmosphere is just fine, making this good, entertaining fun. (Don't mistake the James Mason listed in the cast credits for the famous British actor of the same name.)

LONELY ARE THE BRAVE (1962) B/W. *Dir.:* David Miller. *With:* Kirk Douglas, Walter Matthau, Gena Rowlands, Carroll O'Connor, George Kennedy. **107 mins.** No rating. Beta, VHS **($59.95).** MCA ★★★★

Self-conscious but very effective and moving western starring Douglas as a contemporary cowboy who is alienated by today's modern, mechanized West. Eventually landing in jail,

Douglas escapes and takes to the hills with his horse, Whisky. Pursued by a posse made up of deputies who use helicopters, walkie-talkies, and jeeps, the fugitive cowboy on horseback doesn't stand a chance. The script by Dalton Trumbo is not only poignant but encourages the viewer to think about cowboys, a group of men who were once admired by a society that now can no longer comprehend the values these men represented.

LONG RIDERS, THE (1980) C. *Dir.:* Walter Hill. *With:* James and Stacy Keach; David, Keith, and Robert Carradine; Dennis and Randy Quaid; Christopher and Nicholas Guest; Pamela Reed, James Whitmore, Jr., Harry Carey, Jr. **100 mins.** Rated R. Beta, VHS **($59.95);** CED **($19.98).** MGM/UA. ★★★½

This excellent interpretation of the adventures of Jesse James' notorious gang presents the outlaws as a group of ex-Confederates who refuse to accept that the Civil War is over. They continue to battle the Yankees by robbing the Union's banks and trains. The use of real-life brothers to portray the outlaw brothers (the Keaches play the Jameses, the Carradines play the Youngers) is a unique approach to casting that does not detract from the film as a whole. The slow-motion shoot-outs, the beautiful long shots of the outlaws riding across the grasslands, and the atmospheric scenes of the gang emerging from the foggy night all serve to mythologize the West and its legendary figures. This is one of the richest westerns since *The Wild Bunch* (see review).

LUCKY TERROR (1936) B/W. *Dir.:* Alan James. *With:* Hoot Gibson, Lona Andre, Charles King. **60 mins.** No rating. Beta, VHS **($N/A).** Video Connection. ★★½

A sharp-shooting cowboy joins a medicine show to help a girl whose brother is killed. A breezy, pleasant Hoot Gibson western, with Lona Andre fine as the female lead. It's entertaining but is a must-see only for fans of the Hooter.

LUCKY TEXAN (1934) B/W. *Dir.:* Robert N. Bradbury. *With:* John Wayne, Barbara Sheldon, George "Gabby" Hayes, Yakima Canutt. **61 mins.** No rating. Beta, VHS **($19.95).** Crown, Kartes, Sony, Spotlite. ★★½

Prospectors John Wayne and Gabby Hayes fall into a fortune when they discover a hidden vein of gold. But then Gabby is falsely accused of robbery and murder, and is put in jail. He'll be hanged if Wayne can't find the real killer. Unfortunately, all the evidence points to the sheriff's son as the culprit. Written and directed by Robert N. Bradbury, western star Bob Steele's father, the movie boasts a great finale featuring a railroad-handcar chase. (Sony's tapes are available in Beta Hi-Fi and VHS Hi-Fi.)

LUST IN THE DUST (1984) C. *Dir.:* Paul Bartel. *With:* Tab Hunter, Lainie Kazan, Divine, Geoffrey Lewis, Henry Silva, Cesar Romera, Gina Gallego. **85 mins.** Rated R. Beta, VHS **($79.95);** Laser **($34.95).** New World. ® ★★

Time was when a side of beef in a western meant cattle. Nowadays, it means the ungainly sight of a 300-pound transvestite's naked flanks. Although Divine (the diva in question) seems to be imitating Marlene Dietrich from *Destry Rides Again* in this tinhorn western spoof, the end result is much more like Milton Berle. Former teen idol Tab Hunter plays a Clint Eastwood type—to suitably flaccid effect. The film doesn't know enough about westerns for genre fans to be offended, and the jokes are strictly Catskills. It's not outrageous, but it *is* perverse.

LUSTY MEN, THE (1952) B/W. *Dir.:* Nicholas Ray. *With:* Susan Hayward, Robert Mitchum, Arthur Kennedy, Arthur Hunnicutt. **113 mins.** No rating. Beta, VHS **($39.95).** United. ★★★

Tough rodeo rider Mitchum tries to help aspiring cowboy Kennedy in this hard-hitting western drama. The fine star performances are enhanced by the film's authentic rodeo atmosphere and the realistic behavior of its characters. United's video transfer is scratchy, splicy, and slipshod, an injustice to this fine production.

MAGNIFICENT SEVEN, THE (1960) C. *Dir.:* John Sturges. *With:* Yul Brynner, Steve McQueen, Eli Wallach, James Coburn, Charles Bronson, Robert Vaughn, Horst Buchholz, Brad Dexter. **126 mins.** No rating. Beta, VHS **($59.95);** Laser **($39.98);** CED **($29.98).** CBS/Fox. ★★★★

There's a lot of depth to this post-Civil War tale about how an unlikely bunch of hired guns become a close-knit force for good in the face of injustice. The inhabitants of a Mexican village, finally rebelling against a reign of terror imposed by

The Magnificent Seven

ruthless bandit Calvera (Wallach) and his ruffians, hire gunman Chris (Brynner) to clean out the marauders. Chris in turn recruits five more professional gunmen (McQueen, Coburn, Bronson, Vaughn, and Dexter) and an eager Mexican youth (Buchholz), and the seven go into action. Mutual regard and respect develops between the seven and the villagers, and together they take on Calvera and his gang. This American remake of director Akira Kurosawa's Japanese epic *The Seven Samurai* makes a surprisingly successful marriage between rip-roaring action in the traditional western style and an overall sense of genuine warmth and humanity. The characters of the seven are beautifully scripted as well as beautifully acted. Each performance is a pleasure. It's a thoroughly satisfying movie. Treat yourself to this one.

MAJOR DUNDEE (1965) C. *Dir.:* Sam Peckinpah. *With:* Charlton Heston, Richard Harris, Senta Berger, James Coburn, Jim Hutton, Ben Johnson, Warren Oates. **124 mins.** No rating. Beta, VHS **($59.95);** CED **($29.95).** RCA/Columbia. ★★

Toward the end of the Civil War, Yankee Major Amos Dundee (Heston), commander of an outpost full of Confederate prisoners and assorted undesirables, sets out in pursuit of a renegade Apache gang that has kidnapped some white children. He's aided by a captain (Harris) who had killed a prison guard, but tensions between the two mount—especially when both fall for the same woman (Berger). The expedition is successful, but more adventure awaits the pair. The movie offers some insights into the *modus operandi* of director Peckinpah (*The Wild Bunch*), and reflects his characteristic high-energy approach; but it's confused, confusing, cliché-ridden, and, despite pre-release cuts, overlong. (When the studio recut the film after release, Peckinpah was so unhappy he wanted his name taken off the credits.) The talented cast manage to keep the film afloat—provided the viewer can keep track of the plot.

MAN ALONE, A (1955) C. *Dir.:* Ray Milland. *With:* Ray Milland, Mary Murphy, Ward Bond, Raymond Burr. **96 mins.** No rating. Beta, VHS **($39.95).** Republic. ★★

This was Milland's first outing as a director, and it's okay although Milland seems somewhat miscast. He plays a fugitive gunman who comes to the aid of an invalided sheriff (Bond) and hides out in his house, which is rendered relatively safe by the fact that the sick man is in quarantine. In the course of the story the gunfighter falls in love with the sheriff's daughter and gets to grips with some local criminals. The film is slow, but offbeat enough to make it worth a showing.

MAN CALLED HORSE, A (1970) C. *Dir.:* Elliot Silverstein. *With:* Richard Harris, Judith Anderson, Manu Tupou, Jean Gascon, Corinno Tsopei. **114 mins.** Rated PG. Beta, VHS **($59.95);** CED **($19.98).** CBS/Fox. ★★★

Sportsman Harris, on a hunting expedition in the Old West, survives an Indian attack in which all his men are killed. He's captured and tortured, but wins the admiration of his captors and is made one of the tribe. He even marries one of them. It's an interesting attempt to present the Indians' point of view, but basically it fails to carry conviction. Anderson is good as a Sioux woman. The film is extremely grueling—not for the faint-hearted.

MAN FROM MUSIC MOUNTAIN (1938) B/W. *Dir.:* Joseph Kane. *With:* Gene Autry, Smiley Burnette, Carol Hughes, Sally Payne, Ivan Miller, Polly Jenkins and Her Plowboys. **58 mins.** No rating. Beta, VHS **($19.95).** Kartes. ★★½

Autry and comic sidekick Smiley Burnette help foil a real estate scam in this easy-going musical western. More musical numbers than usual make this B-western somewhat quaint, but performers such as Polly Jenkins and Her Plowboys should pique some viewers' curiosity. This movie has not yet been "officially" made available by Gene Autry. Autry supplies complete, clean prints of his films for video transfer only to Blackhawk. Other companies may have copied their tapes from cut or poor quality prints.

MAN FROM THUNDER RIVER, THE (1943) B/W. *Dir.:* John English. *With:* Bill Elliott, George "Gabby" Hayes, Anne Jeffries, Ian Keith, John James, Georgia Cooper. **57 mins.** No rating. Beta, VHS **($29.95).** Discount. ★★★

"Wild Bill" Elliott helps a girl from being cheated out of her gold ore in this superior, fast-moving Republic western featuring series regulars Gabby Hayes and Anne Jeffries. Along with silent western great William S. Hart, Elliott was one of the best of the B-western stars. Unlike other cowboy actors, Elliott took acting very seriously and maintained a professional attitude toward his work, which undoubtedly accounted for the better quality of his films.

MAN FROM UTAH, THE (1934) B/W. *Dir.:* Robert N. Bradbury. *With:* John Wayne, George "Gabby" Hayes, Polly Ann Young, Yakima Canutt. **55 mins.** No rating. Beta, VHS **($19.95).** Sony, Spotlite. ★★½

A stranger rides into town in the middle of a bank heist and is mistaken for one of the robbers. But since he's played by John Wayne, the accused man is soon cleared and becomes the town's deputy sheriff. He begins investigating a series of mysterious "accidental" deaths and links them to a new rodeo in town. Every man who died had a good chance of winning the rodeo prize money, which has never been collected by anyone not employed by the rodeo owners. Wayne decides to enter the next competition and find out what's going on. An okay actioner with Wayne turning in a credible performance. Polly Ann Young, his female costar, is perhaps best known as the sister of star Loretta Young. (Sony's tapes are available in Beta Hi-Fi and VHS Hi-Fi.)

MAN WHO LOVED CAT DANCING, THE (1973) C. *Dir.:* Richard C. Sarafian. *With:* Burt Reynolds, Sarah Miles, Jack Warden, Lee J. Cobb, George Hamilton, Jay Silverheels. **127 mins.** Rated PG. Beta, VHS **($59.95).** MGM/UA. ★

This movie, which does nothing for the reputation of the western genre, has Miles as a discontented wife who is kid-

The Man From Thunder River

The Man Who Loved Cat Dancing

napped by a bunch of bandits and falls in love with their leader (Reynolds), finding him more exotic than her mining tycoon husband. The scenery is great, which is more than can be said for the plot. Miles is miscast, and the usually ebullient Reynolds appears somewhat downcast. Scriptwriter Eleanor Perry complained at the time that sundry other writers had messed up her script. If so, they didn't do much of a job if all they could produce was this uninspired effort.

MAN WHO SHOT LIBERTY VALANCE, THE (1962) B/W. *Dir.:* John Ford. *With:* James Stewart, John Wayne, Vera Miles, Lee Marvin, Edmond O'Brien, Andy Devine, Woody Strode. **122 mins.** No rating. Beta, VHS **($49.95);** Laser **($29.95);** CED **($19.98).** Paramount. ★★★½

Here's a strongly dramatic, offbeat Ford offering for western fans. Tenderfoot lawyer Stewart arrives in town to set up his practice and promptly gets warned off—by means of a brutal beating—by bad guy Valance (Marvin). Under the care of rancher Wayne, the rancher's sidekick Pompey (Strode), and waitress Miles, the young lawyer recovers and determines to clean up the town. Justice is done, but the wrong man gets credit for the villain's death. A subplot concerns the romantic complications that develop among the three leads, Stewart, Wayne, and Miles. A solid cast strengthens this tale.

MAN WITHOUT A STAR (1955) B/W. *Dir.:* King Vidor. *With:* Kirk Douglas, Jeanne Crain, Claire Trevor, Richard Boone,

Man Without a Star

The Maverick Queen

William Campbell. **89 mins.** No rating. Beta, VHS **($59.95).** MCA. ★★★

Trying to keep one step ahead of the encroachments of civilization (symbolized by the barbed wire that is being used to fence in the formerly wide open spaces), wanderer Dempsey Rae (Douglas) inadvertently gets caught up in the ranch wars. He works for ranch owner Reed Bowman (Crain) until he realizes she's not as nice as he thought, then heads off to town, where he encounters saloon girl Trevor. When he is attacked by the man who has taken over the ranch where he used to work for Bowman, Rae decides to dig in his heels and help the local ranchers protect their property. This is a superior western, tough and with fine action and acting. Watch for Richard Boone (TV's Paladin in *Have Gun Will Travel*) as Miles, the man whose attack prompts Rae to take life seriously for a while.

MARAUDERS, THE (1947) B/W. *Dir.:* George Archainbaud. *With:* Hopalong Cassidy (William Boyd), Rand Brooks, Andy Clyde. **64 mins.** No rating. Beta, VHS **($39.95).** Buena Vista. ★★½

Hopalong and his two sidekicks (Brooks and Clyde) are stuck in a small, deserted town that has fallen prey to a series of threatening incidents. When the village church becomes the next victim, Hoppy vows to help. A typical Hopalong story.

MAVERICK QUEEN, THE (1955) C. *Dir.:* Joseph Kane. *With:* Barbara Stanwyck, Barry Sullivan, Scott Brady, Mary Murphy,

Jim Davis. **90 mins.** No rating. Beta, VHS **($39.95).** Republic. ★★

Pinkerton detective Sullivan sets out to reform saloonkeeper Stanwyck, who is in the unladylike business of heading up a gang of outlaws. He finds his perception of the task in hand skewed by the fact that he falls in love with the woman he's meant to haul before the law. This is a minor Republic drama, but Stanwyck is always worth watching. It's loosely based on a story by Zane Grey, whose writings have been brought to the screen more often than those of any other American writer.

McCABE AND MRS. MILLER (1971) C. *Dir.:* Robert Altman. *With:* Warren Beatty, Julie Christie, Rene Auberjonois, Hugh Millais, Keith Carradine, Shelley Duvall, William DeVane. **120 mins.** Rated R. Beta, VHS **($64.95).** Warner. ★★★★

Warren Beatty gives a fine performance here as drifter and gambler John McCabe, who opens a whorehouse in a turn-of-the-century mining community. The venture is a success, which gets McCabe into trouble with the head honchos of a large mining company who want to unload him and start raking in the takings themselves. Julie Christie won a Best Actress Oscar nomination for her study of the opium-smoking madame with whom McCabe falls in love. Keith Carradine, as a drifter, and Hugh Millais, playing a hired gun, are also very good. This is one of the movies viewers like to argue about. Some praise its poetic feeling and visual beauty; others say it's slow and tedious. Whichever side you're on, it remains another intelligently directed film from Altman, and an interesting application of some of his idiosyncratic techniques to the western form.

MELODY RANCH (1940) B/W. *Dir.:* Joseph Stanley. *With:* Gene Autry, Jimmy Durante, George "Gabby" Hayes, Ann Miller, Barton McLane. **84 mins.** No rating. Beta, VHS **($34.98).** Blackhawk. ★★★½

Gene Autry stars on a radio show called "Melody Ranch," hence the title of this film. He returns to his hometown of Torpedo for Gene Autry Day and ends up battling villain Barton McLane. The movie is one of Gene's best. Republic Studios went all out, giving the film a bigger budget, better production values, and a classier cast than usual. Jimmy Durante, as Autry's joking manager, is especially fun. Don't miss this one.

MELODY TRAIL (1935) B/W. *Dir.:* Joseph Kane. *With:* Gene Autry, Ann Rutherford, Ward Boteler, Smiley Burnette. **60 mins.** No rating. Beta, VHS **($34.98).** Blackhawk. ★★½

Gene Autry plays a champion rodeo rider who loses his winnings to a gypsy thief and is forced to find work fast. He and his pal Frog (Burnette) get jobs as cooks on a dude ranch run by a crew of cowgirls! But things go wrong when the cattle are stolen and a baby is kidnapped. Gene saves the day by capturing both the cattle rustlers and the kidnapper. This is a delightful early Autry film combining comedy, music, and full-blooded action—the kind of mixture that put Gene on top. (The film is also available on a double bill with *Winning of the West* for $39.95 from Republic.)

MISFITS, THE (1961) B/W. *Dir.:* John Huston. *With:* Clark Gable, Marilyn Monroe, Montgomery Clift, Thelma Ritter, Eli Wallach, Kevin McCarthy, Estelle Winwood. **124 mins.** No rating. Beta, VHS **($59.95);** CED **($19.98).** CBS/Fox. ★★★

Playwright Arthur Miller tailored this screenplay for his then wife Marilyn Monroe. It's set in modern Nevada, where divorcee Roslyn Taber (Monroe) pals up with aging cowboy Gay Langland (Gable) who falls in love with her. She also meets his buddy Guido (Wallach) and a washed-up rodeo performer (Clift). These oddly assorted humans, however, are not the "misfits" of the title: The misfits are wild horses, too small for riding, that are being rounded up to be sold for dog food. Guido tries to cut the others in on this roundup scheme, but Roslyn wants to see the animals run free; conflict develops between Roslyn and Gay because Gay is in favor of the roundup. This film, at $4 million the most expensive ever made in black and white, was the last picture for both Monroe and Gable, and the last major picture for Clift. All died soon after the film was finished—in fact, Gable's death occurred only two weeks after shooting ended.

MISSOURIANS, THE (1950) B/W. *Dir.:* George Blair. *With:* Monte Hale, Paul Hurst, Roy Barcroft, Lyn Thomas, Howard J. Negley, Robert Neil. **60 mins.** No rating. Beta, VHS **($29.95).** Discount. ★★★

In the best of the B-westerns that Hale made for Republic Pictures, crooked businessmen try to cheat honest ranchers. Well-paced action scenes make this familiar script stand out.

MISSOURI BREAKS, THE (1976) C. *Dir.:* Arthur Penn. *With:* Marlon Brando, Jack Nicholson, Kathleen Lloyd, Randy Quaid, Harry Dean Stanton, Frederic Forrest. **126 mins.** Rated PG. Beta, VHS **($59.95);** CED **($19.98).** CBS/Fox. ★★

A top-rate cast can't save this disastrous movie about a slightly crazy hired gun (Marlon Brando) who is ordered to get rid of a band of horse thieves (led by Jack Nicholson). To further confuse the issue, the rancher's daughter (Lloyd) has the hots for Nicholson. The story line is muddled and the film doesn't seem to know whose side it's on—neither Brando's nor Nicholson's character is very promising hero material. The acting is good (look for Stanton as Nicholson's sidekick), but the confused plot and excessive violence stamp this one a loser.

MOJAVE FIREBRAND (1944) B/W. *Dir.:* Spencer Bennet. *With:* Bill Elliott, George "Gabby" Hayes, Anne Jeffries, LeRoy Mason, Jack Ingram, Harry McKim, Forrest Taylor, Hal Price. **55 mins.** No rating. Beta, VHS **($N/A).** Nostalgia Merchant. ★★★

Probably the best entry in Elliott's first series for Republic, with veteran B-western director Bennet at the helm. In this oater, Gabby discovers silver and establishes his own town free of crime. Soon, however, bad guy Mason and his gang have introduced corruption into the peaceful community. It is up to Wild Bill Elliott to clean things up. A good example of the entertainment a B-western can provide.

MY PAL TRIGGER (1946) B/W. *Dir.:* Frank McDonald. *With:* Roy Rogers, George "Gabby" Hayes, Dale Evans, Jack Holt, Bob Nolan and the Sons of the Pioneers. **79 mins.** No rating. Beta, VHS **($44.95).** Hollywood Home Theater. ★★★★

My Pal Trigger was Roy Rogers' first A-budget western. It became one of Roy's most popular and successful films—and his own personal favorite. It has fewer songs and silliness than usual, and the strong story focusing on Trigger makes this fine family entertainment. Roy plays a horse trader who meets up with horse breeder Gabby and his daughter (Dale Evans). They clash when Gabby's prized stallion impregnates Roy's mare, and Roy is accused when the stallion is found murdered. He escapes with the mare and her newborn colt, Trigger, and later returns to expose the real culprit, Gabby's rival, a horse breeder and saloon owner (Jack Holt). The movie ends with

Roy and Dale competing in a thrilling horse race. (Prices vary from company to company, but be sure to get the 79-minute, full-length version, not the 54-minute, cut print.)

MYSTERIOUS DESPERADO/RIDER FROM TUCSON (1949/1950) B/W. *Dir.:* Lesley Selander/Lesley Selander. *With:* Tim Holt, Richard Martin, Movita Castenada, Edward Norris/Tim Holt, Richard Martin, Elaine Riley, William Phipps, Veda Ann Borg, Harry Tyler. **121 mins.** No rating. Beta, VHS **($34.95).** RKO. ★★/★★½

After World War II, Tim Holt starred in a series of good, action-packed westerns for RKO. The films featured superior production values and were the studio's only consistent money-makers. Two prime examples are packaged together here. In *Mysterious Desperado*, Holt and his sidekick Chito Gonzales Rafferty (Martin) rescue a murdered man's son (Norris) who has been unjustly accused of a crime. They also expose the corrupt relationship between two crooked land speculators and an unscrupulous official. Ex-Mesquiteer Bob Livingston plays one of the bad guys.

Martin's real-life wife, Elaine Riley, is the heroine in *Rider From Tucson*. She plays a gold miner's (Phipps) fiancée who gets kidnapped by claim jumpers and is rescued by rodeo riders Holt and Martin. Veda Ann Borg is good as the greedy wife of the chief villain (Robert Shaye). The movies make a fun Saturday afternoon double bill.

MYSTERY OF THE HOODED HORSEMAN (1937) B/W. *Dir.:* Ray Taylor. *With:* Tex Ritter, Iris Meredith, Horace Murphy, Charles King, Forrest Taylor. **61 mins.** No rating. Beta, VHS **($24.95).** Discount. ★½

Having made his name on Broadway and on radio, in 1936 Tex Ritter went to Hollywood to star in a series of low-budget westerns for Grand National. He later went on to star in better films for Monogram, Columbia, and Universal while also building up his record career. By the early forties, he had several *Billboard* hits and was often billed as "America's most Beloved Cowboy." But the early musical-westerns Ritter made for Grand National are nothing to boast about. Poor production values make even the better ones, which do not include this one, hard to watch; and Ritter's fine voice is sabotaged by the primitive sound recording.

'NEATH THE ARIZONA SKIES (1934) B/W. *Dir.:* Harry Fraser. *With:* John Wayne, Sheila Terry, Jay Wilsey, George Hayes, Yakima Canutt. **54 mins.** No rating. Beta, VHS **($19.95).** Sony, Spotlite. ★★½

A little Indian girl who stands to inherit a fortune in oil-rich lands is kidnapped by a gang of outlaws who plan to murder her father. It's up to John Wayne, the child's guardian, to find the girl and protect the father. An okay actioner from Wayne's early Republic days. (Sony's tapes are available in Beta Hi-Fi and VHS Hi-Fi.)

NEW FRONTIER, THE (1939). See FRONTIER HORIZON.

NIGHT RIDER, THE (1932) B/W. *Dir.:* William Nigh. *With:* Harry Carey, Eleanor Fair, George Hayes, Julian Rivero, Jack Weatherby, Walter Shumway, Bob Kortman. **72 mins.** No rating. Beta, VHS **($24.95).** Discount. ★

One of several westerns Carey made for producer Louis Weiss in which he was paid $5000 per film. Unfortunately all of them were marred by primitive recording techniques and bad production values. Here Carey, Hayes, and Rivero join forces to track down a mysterious hooded figure. Unless you are a real Carey fan, pass this one up.

NIGHT STAGE TO GALVESTON (1952) B/W. *Dir.:* George Archainbaud. *With:* Gene Autry, Pat Buttram, Virginia Huston, Thurston Hall. **61 mins.** No rating. Beta, VHS **($34.98).** Blackhawk. ★★½

A Galveston newspaper publisher hires ex-Rangers Autry and Buttram to help him expose the corrupt Texas State Police. When the publisher's daughter is kidnapped, it's Gene and Pat to the rescue. Cowboy star Bob Livingston appears in a supporting role. This is one of Autry's later features. The popularity of his films was falling slightly, and he would soon switch to television. However, the quality of his films remained consistently high, with well-written scripts, good production values, and competent acting.

NORTHWEST TRAIL (1946) C. *Dir.:* Derwin Abrahams. *With:* John Litel, Bob Steele, Joan Woodbury, Madge Bellamy, Charles Middleton. **75 mins.** No rating. Beta, VHS **($24.95).** Discount. ★★

A Northwest mountie searches for a killer in this B-western filmed in Cinecolor. Along the way he finds a misunderstood wife who helps him in his quest. This is a fairly good low-budget action yarn with an interesting supporting cast—Bellamy was a well-known silent-film actress and Middleton played Ming the Merciless in the *Flash Gordon* serials.

OKLAHOMA BADLANDS (1948) B/W. *Dir.:* Yakima Canutt. *With:* Allan "Rocky" Lane, Eddy Waller, Mildred Coles, Roy Barcroft, Gene Stutenroth, Earle Hodgins, Dale Van Sickle, House Peters, Jr. **59 mins.** No rating. Beta, VHS **($29.95).** Discount. ★★½

Lane poses as a dude to track down a gang of rustlers in this routine but reliable B-western. Waller provides the comic relief as Lane's sidekick. The film should be of interest to buffs as it marked one of the few times famed stuntman Yakima Canutt served as a full-fledged director. Canutt developed and perfected several stunts that became staples of the western genre and are still in use today. He also was frequently cast in supporting roles, usually as the heavy, and often worked as a second-unit director in charge of action sequences.

OLD BARN DANCE, THE (1938) B/W. *Dir.:* Joseph Kane. *With:* Gene Autry, Smiley Burnette, Helen Valkis, Sammy McKim, Ivan Miller, Earl Dwire, Earle Hodgins, Dick Weston (Roy Rogers), Denver Dixon, The Stafford Sisters, The Maple City Four, Walt Shrum and His Colorado Hillbillies. **60 mins.** No rating. Beta, VHS **($19.95).** Kartes. ★★½

More music than action highlights this lightweight western from Autry's series for Republic Pictures. The format resembles that of the Saturday night radio jamborees popular during the thirties and forties. Here Gene portrays a singing horse-salesman. The music is dated now, but the viewer may find Walt Shrum and His Colorado Hillbillies amusing. Roy Rogers appears in an early role under his first stage name, Dick Weston; his real name is Leonard Slye.

OLD CORRAL, THE (1936) B/W. *Dir.:* Joseph Kane. *With:* Gene Autry, Smiley Burnette, Hope Manning, Cornelius Keefe, Sons of the Pioneers, Lon Chaney, Jr., John Bradford, Abe Lefton, Oscar and Elmer (Ed Platt and Lou Fulton), Milburn Morante. **56 mins.** No rating. Beta, VHS **($19.95).** Kartes, Prism. ★★½

In this unusual western, a sheriff (Autry) is pitted against a group of gangsters from Chicago who want to get rid of a nightclub singer because she can connect them to a murder. Roy Rogers makes a brief appearance as one of the Sons of the Pioneers.

ONCE UPON A TIME IN THE WEST (1968) C. *Dir.:* Sergio Leone. *With:* Henry Fonda, Charles Bronson, Claudia Cardinale, Jason Robards, Keenan Wynn, Jack Elam, Woody Strode. **165 mins.** Rated PG. Beta, VHS **($69.95).** Paramount. ★★★★

Ironically, this, the first spaghetti western filmed in America (much of the footage was shot in Monument Valley), was far more successful financially in Europe and Japan than in the States. It has since gained a significant cult following and is generally considered the best of the spaghetti westerns. With this movie, director Leone wanted to make a statement about America's identification with the mythic Old West, but was misunderstood by critics who felt a non-American filmmaker could not do justice to such an "American" genre. The film's story has to do with a mysterious harmonica player (Bronson), known only as Harmonica, who is on a mission of revenge; his reluctant cohort (Robards); a young widow (Cardinale); and a ruthless gunslinger (Fonda) who plans to kill the widow and take her land. The story really doesn't amount to much, but it doesn't matter. The plot is secondary to the stylized atmosphere and the epic proportions of the west. This is a self-conscious, visually exaggerated study that pays tribute to classic Hollywood westerns by using familiar places and familiar faces. It emphasizes these legendary elements at the expense of action and heroics, and for that reason some viewers may find the movie slow and ponderous. See it if you're an admirer of Leone's earlier work (*A Fistful of Dollars,* etc.). It's interesting, too, for some unusual casting—notably Fonda and Bronson in uncharacteristic roles.

ONE-EYED JACKS (1961) C. *Dir.:* Marlon Brando. *With:* Marlon Brando, Karl Malden, Katy Jurado, Ben Johnson, Pina Pellicer, Slim Pickens, Elisha Cook, Jr. **141 mins.** No rating. Beta, VHS **($72.95).** Paramount. ★★½

Marlon Brando really got his teeth into this psychological western, much to the distress of the studio who had a lot of trouble cutting the movie down to size once Brando was done.

The plot has outlaw Rio (Brando) tracking down former partner Dad Longworth (Malden) who five years earlier made off into the desert with Rio's share of the haul from their bank robberies, leaving Rio to take the heat and go to jail. Dad, however, has switched careers and is now a sheriff. Rio plans to get even by collaborating in a plan to rob the local bank and by seducing Dad's stepdaughter Louisa (an attractive performance from Pellicer). Eventually there's a showdown between Rio and Dad, and Rio rides off into the desert, promising Louisa he'll be back. Brando, who took over direction when Stanley Kubrick cut out, deserves credit for the film's visual power—the photography is impressive. But he's also responsible for the flaws and the fact that the film is so long that getting through it is an exercise in patience on the part of the viewer. (As it is, the viewer is getting off lightly—Brando's original version timed out at some five hours. Brando also went over budget to an awesome degree; the studio planned to spend $1.8 million and wound up spending $6 million.)

100 RIFLES (1969) C. *Dir.:* Tom Gries. *With:* Jim Brown, Raquel Welch, Burt Reynolds, Fernando Lamas. **110 mins.** Rated R. Beta, VHS **($59.95).** CBS/Fox. ★★

A half-breed Yaqui (Reynolds) robs a bank and uses the money to buy rifles in order to arm a downtrodden tribe of Yaqui Indians against an oppressive Mexican army (led by Lamas). An Arizona lawman (Brown) is after Reynolds. This is a well-made, well-photographed actioner that moves along at a pace healthy enough to let you overlook some of its flaws. Reynolds is appealing. There's not much originality here, but it's lively enough to keep you from reaching for the off switch.

ON THE OLD SPANISH TRAIL (1947) B/W. *Dir.:* William Witney. *With:* Roy Rogers, Jane Frazee, Andy Devine, Estelita Rodriguez, Tito Guizar, Bob Nolan and the Sons of the Pioneers. **75 mins.** No rating. Beta, VHS **($N/A).** Video Connection. ★★½

Roy joins a traveling tent show to help the Sons of the Pioneers pay off a debt in this colorful western with a Latin American atmosphere. Supporting actors Guizar and Rodriguez add to the south-of-the-border flavor while Devine provides the comic relief. Be sure to get the more satisfying 75-minute version instead of the shorter version offered by other companies.

On Top of Old Smoky

ON TOP OF OLD SMOKY (1953) B/W. *Dir.:* George Archainbaud. *With:* Gene Autry, Smiley Burnette, Gail Davis, Sheila Ryan. **59 mins.** No rating. Beta, VHS **($39.98).** Blackhawk. ★★½

Gene, the singing star of Gene Autry and His Texas Rangers, is mistaken for a real ranger in this tuneful tale. The songs include "If It Wasn't for the Rain," "I Hang My Head and Cry," "I Saw Her First," "The Trial of Mexico," and, of course, the title song. Straightforward fare from the right-living cowboy. *On Top of Old Smoky* is also available on a double bill with *Prairie Moon* from Republic for $39.95.

OREGON TRAIL (1945) B/W. *Dir.:* Thomas Carr. *With:* Sunset Carson, Peggy Stewart, Frank Jacquet, Si Jenks, John Merton, Mary Carr, Earle Hodgins, Tom London. **55 mins.** No rating. Beta, VHS **($29.95).** Discount. ★★

Low-budget horse opera featuring Carson in his usual role. Carson was never as good an actor as Bob Steele or Bill Elliott and his films frequently feature more action scenes, often lifted from other B-westerns. Die-hard fans will enjoy this entry more than the average viewer.

OREGON TRAIL, THE (1939) B/W. *Dir.:* Ford Beebe. *With:* Johnny Mack Brown, Louise Stanley, Fuzzy Knight, Bill Cody, Jr., Roy Barcroft, Lane Chandler, Jim Thorpe. **195 mins.** No rating. Beta **($55.95);** VHS **($59.95).** Video Connection. ★★

Johnny Mack Brown stars in this western serial comprised of 15 chapters, each chapter approximately 13 minutes long.

He plays the intrepid leader of a wagon train who battles hostile Indians and evil white men to transport the homesteaders in his care to safety.

OREGON TRAIL SCOUTS (1947) B/W. *Dir.:* R.G. Springsteen. *With:* Allan "Rocky" Lane, Bobby Blake, Martha Wentworth, Roy Barcroft, Emmett Lynn, Edmund Cobb, Chief Yowlachie. **58 mins.** No rating. Beta, VHS **($N/A).** Nostalgia Merchant. ★★

It's Red Ryder versus the fur trappers in this formula Republic western. Allan Lane replaced Wild Bill Elliott in the popular series when the latter went on to bigger things. Lane wasn't as popular or as successful as his predecessor in the Ryder role; and after the series, Republic tried to develop Lane as a western star in his own right under the name Rocky Lane. Lane later turned up in the TV series *Mr. Ed* as the voice of the famous talking horse.

OUTLAW, THE (1943) B/W. *Dir.:* Howard Hughes. *With:* Jane Russell, Jack Buetel, Walter Huston, Thomas Mitchell. **103 mins.** No rating. Beta, VHS **($19.95).** Kartes, Prism. ★★½

Howard Hughes' once-controversial western features a curious blend of action and sex. In fact, this offbeat movie offers a prime example of pretty routine material hyped by hysterical publicity. The story has to do with the adventures of Billy the Kid who, wounded and on the run, hides out with (and secretly marries) a sultry half-breed (Russell). The amount of tender loving lavished by Russell upon the worthless outlaw, coupled with her skimpy blouses, so upset the Legion of Decency that, after the movie's 1943 screening, twenty minutes of footage that the Legion found objectionable had to be cut, and the film was not generally released until 1950. It's a telling comment on the times that when the notorious film was re-released in 1976 it was considered suitable family entertainment. The old order changeth. . . . Howard Hughes took over the direction of *The Outlaw* after Howard Hawks walked off the picture because he couldn't work with Hughes. Hughes then proceeded to shoot 470,000 feet of the film—about five times the usual amount—less than a quarter of which made it into the final cut.

OUTLAW JOSEY WALES, THE (1976) C. *Dir.:* Clint Eastwood. *With:* Clint Eastwood, Chief Dan George, Sondra Locke, John

Vernon, Bill McKinney. **135 mins.** Rated PG. Beta, VHS **($59.95).** Warner. ★★★

Eastwood took over direction of this long, arty revenge tale after axing Philip Kaufman shortly after shooting began, thus taking on the triple crown of producer, director, and star. Eastwood's character sees his wife and son murdered by Yankees, joins up with a band of guerrillas, and pursues his quest for vengeance to the end of the Civil War and beyond, felling his enemies right and left. Some of the photography is terrific. Reasonable entertainment for the viewer who doesn't look for too much in the way of character development.

OUTLAW RULE (1935) B/W. *Dir.:* Charles Barton. *With:* Reb Russell, Betty Mack, Yakima Canutt, Jack Rockwell, Al Bridge, Jack Kirk. **60 mins.** No rating. Beta, VHS **($N/A).** Video Connection. ★½

Former football star Reb Russell was a talented athlete, but had no experience in front of a movie camera. He made a series of very low-budget westerns in the thirties of which this is a typical example. Only for die-hard B-western fans or the curious.

OVERLAND MAIL ROBBERY (1943) B/W. *Dir.:* John English. *With:* Bill Elliott, George "Gabby" Hayes, Anne Jeffries, Weldon Heyburn, Nancy Gay, Roy Barcroft, Bud Geary, Jack Kirk, LeRoy Mason, Tom Steele. **56 mins.** No rating. Beta, VHS **($29.95).** Discount. ★★½

Easterner is almost cheated out of his inheritance until Wild Bill helps him. The Republic Wild Bill Elliott westerns were superior entertainment with fine production values and expert fights and action. Gabby Hayes, Anne Jeffries, and Roy Barcroft are plus factors in this one.

PAINTED DESERT, THE (1931) B/W. *Dir.:* Howard Higgins. *With:* William Boyd, Helen Twelvetrees, William Farnum, J. Farrell MacDonald, Clark Gable. **80 mins.** No rating. Beta, VHS **($19.95).** Crown, Kartes. ★★½

Prospectors Cash Holbrook (Farnum) and Jeff Cameron (MacDonald) find an abandoned baby and take him under their wing. Then Cameron adopts the boy, sparking a feud between the two men that's still unresolved when the boy, Bill, is an adult (played by Boyd). In an effort to bring about a reconcilia-

Painted Desert

tion between his adopted father and his one-time friend, Bill woos Holbrook's daughter, Mary Ellen (Twelvetrees). Enter trouble in the person of Brett (Gable) who is sweet on the girl himself, and the two suitors are forced into a confrontation. This old-fashioned curio has some exciting action, but it's notable mainly for giving Gable, as the villain, his first featured movie role and for letting us see Boyd in his pre-Hopalong Cassidy days. The film was remade eight years later with George O'Brien in the Boyd role.

PALE RIDER (1985) C. *Dir.:* Clint Eastwood. *With:* Clint Eastwood, Michael Moriarty, Carrie Snodgress, John Russell, Christopher Penn, Richard Dysart, Sydney Penny, Richard Kiel, Doug McGrath. **113 mins.** Rated R. Beta, VHS **($N/A);** Laser **($N/A).** Warner. ★★★★

Eastwood stars as a nameless stranger who rides out of the mountains to defend a community of prospectors from a mining entrepreneur bent on taking over their claims. The plot of the lone gunfighter who comes from nowhere to single-handedly clean up the town for the benefit of its citizens is a classic western story most effectively used in *Shane* (see review), and also used by Eastwood over a decade ago in his gothic *High Plains Drifter* (see review). The symbolic and religious overtones of *Drifter* are fine-tuned here in *Pale Rider* to add mythic connotations to this film and the western genre in general. The film boasts authentic locales and good performances by the stars and supporting actors, particularly John Russell as the cold-blooded sheriff.

PARADISE CANYON (1935) B/W. *Dir.:* Carl Pierson. *With:* John Wayne, Marion Burns, Earle Hodgins, Yakima Canutt, Reed Howes, Perry Murdock, Gino Corrado. **55 mins.** No rating. Beta, VHS **($19.95).** Sony, Spotlite. ★★½

Just south of the U.S.-Mexico border, a gang of counterfeiters are cranking out phony U.S. currency. Wayne, working undercover for the Treasury Department, is trying to flush out the bad guys, but to do it he has to get the Mexican authorities on his side. Good action to keep the Wayne fans attentive to the end. (Sony's tapes are available in Beta Hi-Fi and VHS Hi-Fi.)

PAROLED—TO DIE (1938) B/W. *Dir.:* Sam Newfield. *With:* Bob Steele, Kathleen Eliot, Karl Hackett, Horace Murphy, Steve Clark, Budd Buster, Sherry Tansey, Frank Ball. **55 mins.** No rating. Beta, VHS **($29.95).** Discount. ★★★

A young rancher is accused of a bank robbery that was actually committed by the banker. But who is going to prove that the rancher didn't do it? Plenty of action to satisfy Steele fans. Steele, son of silent action film director Robert North Bradbury, first appeared on the screen at age 14 with his twin brother in a series of nature shorts directed by the boys' father. He also played juvenile roles in some of his father's westerns, so young Bob was well prepared to embark on a cowboy career of his own.

PAT GARRETT AND BILLY THE KID (1973) C. *Dir.:* Sam Peckinpah. *With:* Kris Kristofferson, James Coburn, Bob Dylan, Jason Robards, Barry Sullivan, Katy Jurado. **106 mins.** Rated R. Beta, VHS **($59.95).** MGM/UA. ★★

Visually striking but disjointed and self-conscious examination of the life and death of Billy the Kid. Exceedingly bloody, too. Against the advice of his friend Pat Garrett (Coburn), Billy refuses to leave the New Mexico Territory. Under sentence of death, Billy escapes from jail and rejoins his old gang at Old Fort Sumner, where Garrett and Poe (Beck) the man appointed by Governor Wallace (Robards) to bring the Kid to justice, finally catch up with him. Peckinpah uses the legend of the Kid—which he'd wanted to film for years—as a symbol of the passing of the ways of the Old West: Times change, but the Kid stays the same. The message, though, doesn't come across (Peckinpah complained that by cutting 15 minutes from the final print, MGM made mincemeat of his story). Coburn and Kristofferson are powerful screen presences, but they can't save this pretentious tale. And many other fine actors are wasted in minor roles. Bob Dylan's soundtrack is no help at all (Dylan also has an acting role here). Where the violence is concerned, Peckinpah pursues his familiar no-holds-barred policy.

PHANTOM EMPIRE, THE (1935) B/W. *Dir.:* Otto Brower and Breezy Reeves Eason. *With:* Gene Autry, Frankie Darro, Betsy King Ross, Dorothy Christie, Smiley Burnette. **245 mins.** No rating. Beta, VHS **($99.95).** Video Yesteryear. ★★

Interesting futuristic western starring the newly discovered singing cowboy Gene Autry. This was a 12-part serial set in a robot-inhabited underground city called Murania (actually, the city was a table-top miniature) led by the evil queen Tika. Autry gets involved in various adventures while battling the Thunder Riders until the hidden city is finally melted by a ray and Autry returns home safely to his ranch, 20,000 feet above the now nonexistent Murania. The movie's theme song, "Silver-Haired Daddy of Mine," became Autry's first hit. Packed with wild action and imaginative cliff-hangers, the serial was later edited, and two features, *Men With Steel Faces* and *Radio Ranch* (see review), were culled from the material.

PHANTOM RANGER (1938) B/W. *Dir.:* Sam Newfield. *With:* Tim McCoy, Suzanne Kaaren, John St. Polis, Charles King. **54 mins.** No rating. Beta, VHS **($24.95).** Discount. ★★

Routine story starring McCoy, made toward the end of his western career and in the same year he launched his own unsuccessful Wild West show. In 1940 he was back on the

Phantom Ranger

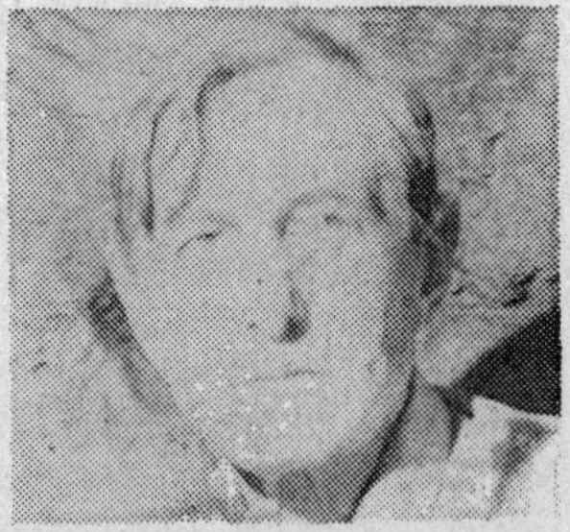
Powdersmoke Range

screen in the "Rough Riders" series, which was halted in 1942 when costar Buck Jones died in a fire. After World War II, McCoy retired to his ranch in Wyoming, although he did resume acting several years later and was seen both on TV and in movies. McCoy died in 1973.

PHANTOM THUNDERBOLT, THE (1933) B/W. *Dir.:* Alan James. *With:* Ken Maynard, Frances Dade, Frank Rice, William Gould, Bob Kortman. **63 mins.** No rating. Beta, VHS **($24.95).** Discount. ★★

Maynard rides again in this movie that he made in mid-career when his popularity was still high. Maynard, a former rodeo rider, was a favorite with youngsters (along with his famous horse Tarzan) in the days of the silents, and he took the talkies in his stride. Maynard, in fact, was singing in westerns a couple of years before Gene Autry, who's generally thought of as the first singing cowboy. During the thirties Maynard's star began to fall, and by 1940 he was riding rodeos once more. He turns in a creditable performance in this film.

PIONEER MARSHAL (1949) B/W. *Dir.:* Philip Ford. *With:* Monte Hale, Nan Leslie, Paul Hurst, Roy Barcroft. **60 mins.** No rating. Beta, VHS **($29.95).** Discount. ★★

So-so offering from Republic has Monte Hale don his cowboy boots once more to find adventure in an outlaw town. Not bad, but there are plenty of better B-westerns around. See it only if you're a fan of the star.

POCATELLO KID, THE (1931) B/W. *Dir.:* Phil Rosen. *With:* Ken Maynard, Marceline Day, Dick Cramer, Charles King. **60 mins.** No rating. Beta, VHS **($24.95).** Discount. ★★½

Maynard does double duty here as a gunman who is shot down while trying to escape, and the cowboy who assumes the dead man's identity. Solid, old-fashioned western with sufficient action to hold the attention of fans of the genre. Enjoyable for those with a taste for vintage westerns.

POWDERSMOKE RANGE (1935) B/W. *Dir.:* Wallace Fox. *With:* Harry Carey, Hoot Gibson, Bob Steele, Tom Tyler, Guinn "Big Boy" Williams, William Farnum, William Desmond, Patricia "Boots" Mallory. **71 mins.** No rating. Beta, VHS **($N/A).** Nostalgia Merchant. ★★½

Advertised as "The Greatest Roundup of Western Stars in History," this movie brought together a great cast of cowboy stars of the thirties and, into the bargain, sparked the "Three Mesquiteers" series. So it's a must for all B-western fans. The story doesn't much matter since the pulling power lies in the cast; but for the record, the trio thwart a plot to frame them for a stagecoach robbery, and there's a good gunfight to keep the action moving. The Mesquiteers here are Carey, Gibson, and Williams, and it's interesting to note that for one of the eight movies in the series John Wayne took over the Carey role. The leading lady, Patricia "Boots" Mallory, was the wife of actor Herbert Marshall. See this one for the stars.

PRAIRIE MOON (1938) B/W. *Dir.:* Ralph Staub. *With:* Gene Autry, Smiley Burnette, Tommy Ryan, David Gorcey, Peter Potter. **58 mins.** No rating. Beta, VHS **($34.98).** Blackhawk. ★★★

Rancher-cum-gangster shows up in town to see his storekeeper partner, who double-crosses him. The rancher is killed in a shoot-out, first making Autry's character promise to care for his three sons. Fine action and pleasant songs make this a satisfying movie. Autry sings "He's in the Jailhouse Now" and Burnette's big number is "The Story of Trigger Joe." The cast includes David Gorcey, brother of actor Leo. *Prairie Moon* is also available on a double bill with *On Top of Old Smoky* for $39.95 from Republic.

PROFESSIONALS, THE (1966) C. *Dir.:* Richard Brooks. *With:* Burt Lancaster, Lee Marvin, Jack Palance, Robert Ryan, Claudia Cardinale, Woody Strode, Ralph Bellamy. **117 mins.** Rated PG. Beta, VHS **($59.95).** RCA/Columbia. ★★★

Mercenaries Lancaster, Marvin, Ryan, and Strode are hired by wealthy J. W. Grant (Bellamy) to rescue his wife, Maria (Cardinale), who has been kidnapped by Mexican bandit Captain Jesus Raza (Palance). Grant reckons he's got a can't-lose rescue team because each of the four has a specialty—Lancaster, for instance, knows all about explosives, and Strode's a tracker—so their combined skills are pretty impressive. Grant is correct in his assumption. The rescuers do indeed find Maria, but also learn that she's singularly ungrateful for their efforts. She'd rather stay with her abductor, and when the quartet realizes why—Grant is actually a heel—they side

The Professionals

with Maria and conspire to get her and Raza together again. This is splendid entertainment, full of noise and action and generally a rollicking all-around audience pleaser. Bear with the bits where the adventurers slow down the action by getting overphilosophical; the story soon gets moving again. Director Brooks received an Oscar nomination for this film.

PROUD REBEL, THE (1958) C. *Dir.:* Michael Curtiz. *With:* Alan Ladd, Olivia de Havilland, David Ladd, Dean Jagger. **99 mins.** No rating. Beta, VHS **($69.95).** Embassy. ★★★

This somewhat derivative but still superior yarn features Alan Ladd as a former Confederate soldier whose son has been so traumatized by the war that he is unable to speak. Ladd takes the boy (played by his own son David) to find a doctor who may be able to cure him. In the course of their pilgrimage they meet spinster rancher De Havilland (who came out of voluntary retirement to do the part), and get mixed up with the family of land-grabbing louts who are hounding her. Solid fare, and livelier than you might expect. De Havilland is lovely.

PUBLIC COWBOY NO. 1 (1937) B/W. *Dir.:* Joseph Kane. *With:* Gene Autry, William Farnum, Smiley Burnette, Ann Rutherford. **54 mins.** No rating. Beta, VHS **($N/A).** Video Connection. ★★★½

Rustlers employ modern methods, including hijacking trucks, in their efforts to outwit ranchers. This is a fast-moving, action-packed musical western with silent great Farnum in a good role. Plenty of charm from Autry.

PURPLE VIGILANTES, THE (1938) B/W. *Dir.:* George Sherman. *With:* Bob Livingston, Ray Corrigan, Max Terhune, Joan Barclay, Jack Perrin. **54 mins.** No rating. Beta, VHS **($29.95).** Discount. ★★★

The Three Mesquiteers infiltrate a gang of hooded killers. Strong action and a good story make this one of the best of the earlier films in the series. The Mesquiteers here are Livingston, Corrigan, and Terhune.

RACHEL AND THE STRANGER (1948) B/W. *Dir.:* Norman Foster. *With:* William Holden, Robert Mitchum, Loretta Young, Gary Gray. **93 mins.** No rating. Beta, VHS **($N/A).** Nostalgia Merchant. ★★★

Satisfying, folksy tale that centers on an 1820s bondswoman (Young) who is bought for "$18 and $4 owing" by backwoods widower Holden because he needs help on his farm. For the sake of propriety he marries her, also hoping that she'll be a good influence on his unruly son (Gray). Both men, however, treat the poor girl shabbily, and it's not until family friend Mitchum tries to buy her for himself that Holden realizes that he has come to love the wife he married for convenience. Young gives a beautiful portrayal of the servant who longs to receive respect for her personal dignity, and Holden handles very well his character's transition from unfeeling clod to loving husband. An Indian attack injects action into the somewhat talky movie. An unusually thoughtful western that takes the trouble to get inside its characters.

RACKETEERS OF THE RANGE (1939) B/W. *Dir.:* D. Ross Lederman. *With:* George O'Brien, Marjorie Reynolds, Chill Wills. **62 mins.** No rating. Beta, VHS **($N/A).** Nostalgia Merchant. ★★★

Meat-packing crooks rustle cattle using modern methods. Here's a top-notch, crackling O'Brien western with lots of action. Watch for the exciting scene in which O'Brien jumps from his horse to a moving train—without using a double! The supporting cast, which includes singer Ray Whitely, keeps things moving right along. Excellent bet for B-western buffs.

RADIO RANCH (1935) B/W. *Dir.:* Otto Brower and Breezy Reeves Eason. *With:* Gene Autry, Frankie Darro, Betsy King Ross, Smiley Burnette. **71 mins.** No rating. Beta, VHS **($49.95).** Video Yesteryear. ★

Autry's powerful appeal is poorly served by this haphazard compilation from his serial *The Phantom Empire* (see review), in which the cowboy explores the hidden, underground city of Murania, which is bent on disrupting the harmony at Autry's Radio Ranch. Choppy editing, crude production values, and poor sound make this a movie that all but diehard Autry fans can take a pass on. The serial is better than this version.

RAIDERS OF RED GAP (1934) B/W. *Dir.:* Sam Newfield. *With:* Bob Livingston, Al "Fuzzy" St. John, Myrna Dell, Charles King, Slim Whitaker, Kermit Maynard. **56 mins.** No rating. Beta, VHS **($39.95).** Video Yesteryear. ★

Another cheapie western from PRC Productions. In this one, the Bennett Cattle Company tries to drive off homesteaders in order to get control of their land; Fuzzy is mistaken for the gunfighter hired by the crooked company; and "The Lone Rider" (Livingston) saves the day. Nothing special.

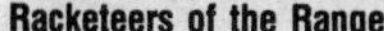

Racketeers of the Range

Raiders of Red Gap

RAIDERS OF SAN JOAQUIN (1943) B/W. *Dir.:* Lewis Collins. *With:* Johnny Mack Brown, Tex Ritter, Fuzzy Knight, Jennifer Holt, Jimmy Wakely Trio. **60 mins.** No rating. Beta, VHS **($24.95).** Discount. ★★½

In this pleasant Universal western, Brown and Ritter battle an unscrupulous land baron. Not bad entertainment. The music, horsemanship, fights, and production values in Universal oaters like this one are always superior to those in the stars' independent efforts. Here, Knight provides the laughs and Holt the glamour.

RAINBOW'S END (1933) B/W. *Dir.:* Norman Spencer. *With:* Hoot Gibson, June Gale, Buddy Roosevelt, Oscar Apfel. **60 mins.** No rating. Beta, VHS **($N/A).** Video Connection. ★★½

Big-city gangsters head west but find they are no match for a fighting cowboy. This is a typical Hoot Gibson independent with breezy action and comedy. If you like Gibson's movies or are curious and want to try one, you could do a lot worse than this.

RANCHO NOTORIOUS (1952) C. *Dir.:* Fritz Lang. *With:* Marlene Dietrich, Arthur Kennedy, Mel Ferrer. **89 mins.** No rating. Beta, VHS **($N/A).** United. ★★★

Dietrich plays an ex-saloon singer operating a hideout for outlaws in this attractive Technicolor curiosity. Dramatic conflict is engaged with the arrival of Kennedy, who seeks revenge on the rapist who killed his fiancée. Lang's icy handling of such passionate material is unusual enough to captivate, and the sterling cast and excellent supporting talent—including Jack Elam, George Reeves, and William Frawley—make this enjoyable viewing throughout.

RANDY RIDES ALONE (1934) B/W. *Dir.:* Harry Fraser. *With:* John Wayne, Alberta Vaughn, George Hayes, Yakima Canutt. **53 mins.** No rating. Beta, VHS **($19.95)**. Sony, Spotlite. ★★★

This good mystery-western has Wayne discovering a saloon full of murdered patrons and then being accused of killing them himself. He's jailed, but escapes and sets off to bring the real villains to justice and so clear his own name. This is a strange and offbeat film with some interesting plot twists. Hayes, Canutt, and silent screen leading lady Vaughn give staunch support. (Sony's tapes are available in Beta Hi-Fi and VHS Hi-Fi.)

RANGE BUSTERS, THE (1940) B/W. *Dir.:* Lambert Hillyer. *With:* Ray Corrigan, John King, Max Terhune, LeRoy Mason, Luana Walters, Kermit Maynard. **55 mins.** No rating. Beta, VHS **($24.95).** Discount. ★★

Monogram's attempt to copy Republic's "Three Mesquiteers" series resulted in a series of cheaply made minor action films that were vastly inferior to the originals. This is one of the inferior copies. Corrigan, Terhune, and King are in this one (the third member of the trio would change now and again). Leading lady Walters offers some reward for sitting through this nonsense.

RANGE LAW (1931) B/W. *Dir.:* Phil Rosen. *With:* Ken Maynard, Frances Dade, Charles King, Frank Mayo, Lafe McKee. **63 mins.** No rating. Beta, VHS **($24.95).** Discount. ★

One of Maynard's pictures for minimum-budget Tiffany Productions. It's an awful bore even though it features Tarzan, the best horse in motion pictures. Tarzan was also the first horse to receive screen credit. Maynard began his career using other horses, but in the mid-1920s, he bought the soon-to-be-famous palomino for $50 and named him after Edgar Rice Burrough's jungle hero. After that, Maynard used the easily trained Tarzan almost exclusively, and Maynard's films depended heavily on horse action. Unfortunately, Tiffany did not have the money necessary to stage exciting action sequences, keeping Ken and Tarzan from performing all but the usual stunts here. If you want to see them in top form, watch *Come On, Tarzan* instead.

Red River

RED RIVER (1948) B/W. *Dir.:* Howard Hawks. *With:* John Wayne, Montgomery Clift, Walter Brennan, Joanne Dru, John Ireland. **125 mins.** No rating. Beta, VHS **($59.98);** CED **($29.98).** Key. ★★★★

A ruthless Texas cattle baron (Wayne) is obsessed with building an empire. When his harsh methods drive his men and his adopted son (Clift) to rebel, he vows to kill the boy. Wayne delivers one of his finest performances here, and this is one of the greatest westerns ever filmed—a magnificent, large-scale epic that may be Hawks' all-time best. This film is given additional resonance and depth by Russell Harlan's evocative black-and-white photography, which is suffused with an almost painfully nostalgic glow.

RED RIVER RENEGADES (1946) B/W. *Dir.:* Thomas Carr. *With:* Sunset Carson, Peggy Stewart, Bruce Langley, Tom London, LeRoy Mason. **55 mins.** No rating. Beta, VHS **($29.95).** Discount. ★★½

A postal inspector fights counterfeiters in this okay actioner from Republic. Carson (who was born Michael Harrison but changed his name to that of the character he was to play in a series of Republic westerns) is always good for plenty of fights and thrills. The female lead is former teen star Stewart, who played opposite many top cowboys of the thirties and married (and later divorced) one of them, Don "Red" Barry.

RETURN OF A MAN CALLED HORSE, THE (1976) C. *Dir.:* Irvin Kershner. *With:* Richard Harris, Gale Sondergaard, Jorge Luke, Geoffrey Lewis. **125 mins.** Rated PG. Beta, VHS **($59.98).** CBS/Fox. ★½

English sportsman Harris is once more on the side of the Sioux—who made him one of their own in the 1969 original (see *A Man Called Horse*)—against both white and Indian exploiters. This is not much more than a rehash of the original, and there's not much to excite the audience except an effective and moving portrayal of a buffalo hunt. Gale Sondergaard (as an old Indian woman) makes a welcome return to the screen after being blacklisted for many years, but she's worth better material than she's offered here. Abundant violence will turn off sensitive viewers. In fact, there's not much motivation for any viewer to return to this one.

RETURN OF THE BAD MEN (1948) B/W. *Dir.:* Ray Enright. *With:* Randolph Scott, Robert Ryan, Anne Jeffries, George "Gabby" Hayes, Jason Robards, Sr. **90 mins.** No rating. Beta, VHS **($34.98).** Blackhawk. ★★★

An outlaw gang interferes with a peaceful man's attempt to stake a claim during the Oklahoma land rush and to marry the sheriff's widow. This superior grade-A western has enough rip-roaring action to keep the fans satisfied, and there's a fine performance from Ryan. This was a sequel to *Badmen's Territory* and was in turn followed by the lesser *Best of the Badmen.*

RIDE IN THE WHIRLWIND (1967) C. *Dir.:* Monte Hellman. *With:* Jack Nicholson, Cameron Mitchell, Millie Perkins, Katherine Squire. **83 mins.** No rating. Beta, VHS **($39.95).** Media. ★★

This is a somewhat pretentious attempt to bring psychological interpretations to bear on the tale of young cowboys on the run from a posse that has them tagged, wrongly, as members of an outlaw gang. An interesting cast turns in some fine acting, but it's hard to find much else to justify the cult status acquired by this less-than-satisfying movie. It's worthy of note that Nicholson and Hellman coproduced two mini-budget westerns—this and *The Shooting* (see review)—before Nicholson hit the big time with *Easy Rider*. Both were released in Europe several years before they were seen in the States.

RIDER FROM TUCSON. See MYSTERIOUS DESPERADO/RIDER FROM TUCSON.

RIDERS OF DEATH VALLEY (1941) B/W. *Dir.:* Ford Beebe and Ray Taylor. *With:* Buck Jones, Lon Chaney, Jr., Dick Foran, Leo Carillo, Charles Bickford, Noah Beery, Jr. **195 mins.** No rating. Beta, VHS **($N/A).** Video Connection. ★★½

Advertised as a "Million Dollar Serial," this actually offers fairly routine action adventure. The big story is the lineup of stars—including Bickford, who was one of the few major performers who appeared as a villain in a serial. This series of 13 short episodes has Jones (in his fifth and last serial for Universal) as a member of a vigilante group trying to break up a protection racket whose members are trying to take over mining claims. Interesting for gathering so many big names in the same place at the same time.

RIDERS OF DESTINY (1933) B/W. *Dir.:* Robert N. Bradbury. *With:* John Wayne, George "Gabby" Hayes, Cecilia Parker, Forrest Taylor, Al "Fuzzy" St. John, Yakima Canutt. **57 mins.** No rating. Beta, VHS **($19.95).** Sony, Spotlite. ★★★

A battle for water rights is the crux of this action-packed western. A gang has a stranglehold on the local water supply,

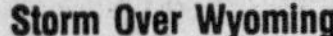

Storm Over Wyoming

Ride the Man Down

and Wayne has to infiltrate the bad guys before he can figure out a way to trick them into releasing their grip. Parker turns in a creditable performance as the heroine. (Sony's tapes are available in Beta Hi-Fi and VHS Hi-Fi.)

RIDERS OF THE RANGE/STORM OVER WYOMING (1949/1950) B/W. *Dir.:* Lesley Selander/Lesley Selander. *With:* Tim Holt, Richard Martin, Jacqueline White, Tom Tyler/Tim Holt, Richard Martin, Noreen Nash, Richard Powers (Tom Keene). **120 mins.** No rating. Beta, VHS **($34.95).** RKO. ★★½/★★★

In *Riders of the Range* Holt and sidekick Martin save a rancher's (White) no-good brother from a crooked gambler and end up working for the grateful lady rancher. The action builds when the two men are framed for murder and must find the real killer in order to prove their own innocence. Not bad.

Storm Over Wyoming displays the Holt-Martin partnership at its best. The two play roving cowboys who break up a lynching, thus getting in the hair of the mean sheep owner (Bill Kennedy) who organized the incident (and others like it) in order to mask his own shady goings-on. There's a terrific sequence where Holt, in close-up and without a stunt double, leaps from his horse to the runaway wagon he's trying to save. Lots of worthwhile entertainment in a well-matched double bill.

RIDERS OF THE WEST (1942) B/W. *Dir.:* Howard Bretherton. *With:* Buck Jones, Tim McCoy, Raymond Hatton, Sarah Padden, Dennis Moore, Harry Woods, Kermit Maynard. **58 mins.** No rating. Beta, VHS **($N/A).** Video Connection. ★★½

Cattle rustlers are on the prowl again and it takes the

Rough Riders to round them up. The story doesn't matter—the entertainment is in watching those grand old-timers Jones, McCoy, and Hatton. Their fans will lap this up.

RIDERS OF THE WHISTLING SKULL (1937) B/W. *Dir.:* Mack V. Wright. *With:* Bob Livingston, Ray Corrigan, Max Terhune, Mary Russell, Yakima Canutt, Roger Williams. **54 mins.** No rating. Beta, VHS **($N/A).** Video Connection. ★★½

This rather unusual western has the Three Mesquiteers plonked in the middle of an archaeological expedition in search of a lost Indian tribe. There's also a search going on for an archaeologist who's gone AWOL in a remote area of the Painted Desert. Fern Emmett, as the man-hungry aunt of the heroine (Russell), provides much of the comedy here. The title, incidentally, refers to a rock formation that guards the entrance to the lost city and makes a whistling noise when the wind's in the right direction. We thought you'd like to know.

RIDE THE MAN DOWN (1953) C. *Dir.:* Joseph Kane. *With:* Rod Cameron, Ella Raines, Brian Donlevy, Barbara Britton, Forrest Tucker, J. Carrol Naish, Jim Davis, Chill Wills. **90 mins.** No rating. Beta, VHS **($39.95).** Republic. ★★

Ranch foreman Cameron helps rancher's daughter Raines protect her homestead after her father's death. Land grabbers Donlevy and Tucker and rustler Davis are all after the dead man's property. Both Raines and town girl Britton are after Cameron, romantically speaking. This is standard upper-budget Republic fare that offers good entertainment value for western buffs. The film, based on Luke Short's novel, has few pretensions, but a well-chosen cast gives it class. Watch for screen gangster Jack LaRue in a bit role.

RIDIN' ON A RAINBOW (1941) B/W. *Dir.:* Lew Landers. *With:* Gene Autry, Smiley Burnette, Mary Lee, Carol Adams, Ferris Taylor. **74 mins.** No rating. Beta, VHS **($34.98).** Blackhawk. ★★★½

Has-been Matt Evans, father of a small daughter, works on a paddlewheel steamer. He's persuaded to join an upcoming bank robbery, hoping that his share of the take will buy a new start for him and his little girl. Our heroes, of course, ride up to straighten everything out. The novel setting, fine action, and pleasant music add up to exciting entertainment. Worth seeing.

RIDING THE CALIFORNIA TRAIL (1947) B/W. *Dir.:* William Nigh. *With:* Gilbert Roland, Martin Garralaga, Frank Yaconelli, Teala Loring, Inez Cooper. **59 mins.** No rating. Beta, VHS **($24.95).** Discount. ★★

Roland exudes self-confidence as the Cisco Kid in this low-budget Monogram production. He gets good support from solid character actors Garralaga and Yaconelli. Roland himself is best known as the Latin lover who showed up regularly in silent movies breaking women's hearts. Born Luis Antonio Damaso de Alonso, son of a bullfighter, Roland also trained for the ring before turning to acting as a way of life. A movie he made in 1951, *The Bullfighter and the Lady*, must have stirred up many memories of his pre-screen ambitions.

Riding the California Trail

Rio Bravo

RIO BRAVO (1959) C. *Dir.:* Howard Hawks. *With:* John Wayne, Dean Martin, Angie Dickinson, Ricky Nelson, Walter Brennan. **140 mins.** No rating. Beta, VHS **($59.95)**; CED **($29.98).** Warner. ★★★½

This good-natured western focuses on the plight of John T. Chance (Wayne), an aging sheriff who must defend his jail against a siege by his prisoner's gang, aided only by drunken gunfighter Martin, green kid Nelson, elderly cripple Brennan, and seductive gambler Dickinson. As with many of his later films, some of the scenes in this archetypal Hawks movie are leisurely paced, and the cheap studio sets are often unconvincing. Still, there's an unquestionable air of tension, which builds to an exciting climax, and the performances are surprisingly good. All in all, it's an enjoyable western. Hawks liked the story so much that he used it again in 1967 for *El Dorado*.

RIO GRANDE (1950) B/W. *Dir.:* John Ford. *With:* John Wayne, Maureen O'Hara, Ben Johnson, Victor McLaglen, Claude Jarman, Jr. **105 mins.** No rating. Beta, VHS **($39.95).** Republic. ★★★½

This magnificent final entry in Ford's famous "cavalry trilogy" finds Wayne and O'Hara as a couple who meet after a long separation when their son (Jarman, the boy in *The Yearling*) joins his father's command post. O'Hara wants Wayne to agree to Jarman's discharge, but Wayne refuses and their estrangement continues. They finally settle their differences when they face a war with the Apaches. The domestic angle provides a welcome freshness to the film's rather commonplace scenes of preparing for battle, training recruits, etc. The sparkling chemistry between the two stars led to their being reteamed many more times—most notably in Ford's *The Quiet Man*.

RIO GRANDE RAIDERS (1946) B/W. *Dir.:* Thomas Carr. *With:* Sunset Carson, Linda Stirling, Bob Steele, Tom London, Tris Coffin. **56 mins.** No rating. Beta, VHS **($29.95).** Discount. ★★½

The owners of rival stagecoach lines fight it out. This is a reliable Sunset Carson western from Republic. It's helped by an above-average performance from Steele and good support from leading lady Stirling.

RIO LOBO (1970) C. *Dir.:* Howard Hawks. *With:* John Wayne, Jorge Rivero, Jennifer O'Neill, Jack Elam, Christopher Mitchum. **114 mins.** Rated G. Beta, VHS **($49.95)**; CED **($19.98).** CBS/Fox. ★★★

Ex-Union officer Wayne has a chip on his shoulder and a few scores to settle. He rides off to settle them in the company of a Confederate leader (Rivero) and his sergeant (Mitchum), who had been prisoners in Wayne's charge and were grateful enough for his good treatment of them to join him on his mission. This old-fashioned but pleasing Wayne vehicle has fine action, a number of first-rate performances (although some of the supporting actors are weak), an appealing heroine in Jennifer O'Neill (who would show up to better effect in the 1971 movie *Summer of '42*), and some wonderful funny moments from Jack Elam. It also gave Wayne a chance to prove that as an actor he was by no means ready to ride off into the sunset. Wayne fans will love it. A couple of cast notes: The supporting cast includes producer and former studio head Sherry Lansing in her performing days. Robert Mitchum was offered a costarring role but turned it down because he didn't like the part.

ROBIN HOOD OF TEXAS (1947) B/W. *Dir.:* Lesley Selander. *With:* Gene Autry, Sterling Holloway, Lynne Roberts, Adele Mara, Cass County Boys. **71 mins.** No rating. Beta, VHS **($34.98).** Blackhawk. ★★½

In his last film for Republic, Gene and dude ranch visitors are robbed and locked in a storage room. Gene helps them all escape and then goes after the bad guys. Great action, lots of hard riding, and enough entertainment value to make this a worthy exit for Autry. It's even positively symbolic—the good guys wear white; the bad guys wear black. No excuse for not knowing who is on which side here. Good music from the Cass County Boys.

ROLL ALONG, COWBOY (1937) B/W. *Dir.:* Gus Meins. *With:* Smith Ballew, Cecilia Parker, Stanley Fields, Gordon (Wild Bill) Elliott, Guster Fite and His Six Saddle Tramps. **55 mins.** No rating. Beta, VHS **($19.98).** Blackhawk. ★

Ballew and sidekick Fields are cowhands employed by a lady rancher. When the ranch begins to have severe financial problems, most of the other hands leave to work for the unscrupulous rival rancher. Ballew, who is in love with the rancher's daughter, and Fields decide to stay and help out. Independent producer Sol Lesser tried in vain to make a successful singing cowboy out of lanky Smith Ballew (who dubbed John Wayne's singing voice in several early westerns). Unfortunately, Lesser didn't have the expert know-how of the producers at Republic Studios or Universal Pictures, and Ballew lacked the charm or talent of other singing cowboys.

ROLL ON, TEXAS MOON (1946) B/W. *Dir.:* William Witney. *With:* Roy Rogers, George "Gabby" Hayes, Dale Evans, Bob Nolan and the Sons of the Pioneers. **68 mins.** No rating. Beta, VHS **($24.95).** Discount. ★★½

A range war rages between the cattlemen and the sheep herders. The plot is familiar (and so is the cast), but some lively action and a few songs help keep things moving. This was the first of 27 films director Witney made with Rogers, and it rolls on amiably enough.

ROMANCE ON THE RANGE. See TRAIL OF ROBIN HOOD/ ROMANCE ON THE RANGE.

Rooster Cogburn

ROOSTER COGBURN (1975) C. *Dir.:* Stuart Miller. *With:* John Wayne, Katharine Hepburn, John McIntire, Richard Jordan, Anthony Zerbe, Strother Martin. **107 mins.** Rated PG. Beta. VHS **($39.95).** MCA. ★★

Now here's a potentially fascinating bit of casting—John Wayne teamed with Katharine Hepburn in a sequel to the popular *True Grit* (see review). Talk about covering all the bases at the box office. All the folks concerned probably thought they were making a great western. Unfortunately, however, the movie magicians blew this clever trick. The film relies far too heavily on the drawing power of the stars (and is extremely indulgent toward them) at the expense of a solid plot or a tight structure. Wayne and Hepburn are planted firmly center stage, but given very little material on which to build a starring act. The plot concerns a missionary (Hepburn) and a hard-drinking, trigger happy U.S. Marshal (Wayne) who has lost his badge for shooting down three outlaws he was supposed to bring in alive. The unlikely couple join up in a search for the killer of Hepburn's parents. Eventually Hepburn, who has fallen in love with her rugged cohort, gets Wayne's status as Marshal restored. Wayne's character is basically unattractive (he was to fare much better in *The Shootist*), and the weak story draws too obviously on the early Hepburn/Bogart star vehicle *The*

African Queen (1951)—witness the scene where the two leads take the rapids on a raft. The film is good-looking, and it has curiosity value, but don't expect a great western—or, for that matter, a great movie of any kind.

ROUGH RIDERS OF CHEYENNE (1945) B/W. *Dir.:* Thomas Carr. *With:* Sunset Carson, Peggy Stewart, Mira McKinney, Monte Hale, Wade Crosby. **54 mins.** No rating. Beta, VHS **($29.95).** Discount. ★★½

A cowboy tries to settle a family feud after his brother's death in this predictable but adequate Sunset Carson western for Republic. No great shakes, but it moves along at a fairly steady pace. Watch for former minor star Jack Luden, and an appearance by Hale before he started his own series. Stewart is a likable leading lady.

ROUGH RIDERS' ROUNDUP (1939) B/W. *Dir.:* Joseph Kane. *With:* Roy Rogers, Mary Hart (Lynne Roberts), Raymond Hatton, Eddie Acuff, Duncan Renaldo. **60 mins.** No rating. Beta, VHS **($24.95).** Discount. ★★

This fairly entertaining low-budget tale is one of Rogers' early efforts. Here he and his rough-riding pals round up the bad guys. There's competent assistance from Hart, Hatton, and some well-known old-timers. A pleasant enough way to pass the time, but don't expect a lot of excitement.

RUN OF THE ARROW (1956) C. *Dir.:* Samuel Fuller. *With:* Rod Steiger, Brian Keith, Ralph Meeker, Charles Bronson, Sarita Montiel, Jay C. Flippen, Col. Tim McCoy. **85 mins.** No rating. Beta, VHS **($N/A).** United. ★★★

Former Confederate private Steiger joins the Sioux Indians in this unusual film that treats the Indians with rare sympathy. Steiger is oddly cast, and this noted performer's Method-ology makes for some strained moments—there's altogether more actor here than the film demands. In contrast, Keith's handling of his part as a cavalry officer is much more satisfying. This is a very well photographed film, but the heavy-handed treatment makes it heavy going for the viewer, and although there's action aplenty, there's plenty of violence, too. Strong stuff, and of interest to fans of offbeat westerns, but altogether overdone. Latin American star Sarita Montiel is an asset, and western great Tim McCoy puts in an appearance.

SAGA OF DEATH VALLEY (1939) B/W. *Dir.:* Joseph Kane. *With:* Roy Rogers, George "Gabby" Hayes, Donald Barry, Doris Day. **56 mins.** No rating. Beta, VHS **($N/A).** Nostalgia Merchant. ★★★

Outstandingly beautiful nighttime photography lifts this low-budget early Rogers film right out of the rut and compensates for a pretty ho-hum plot about a cattle town and its water supply. Watch for the comfortingly familiar presence of Gabby Hayes. Don "Red" Barry puts in an appearance too. The Doris Day listed in the credits is not the one you're thinking of.

SAGEBRUSH TRAIL, THE (1933) B/W. *Dir.:* Armand Schaefer. *With:* John Wayne, Lane Chandler, Nancy Shubert, Wally Wales, Yakima Canutt, Art Mix. **60 mins.** No rating. Beta, VHS **($19.95).** Sony, Spotlite. ★★★

A cowboy jailed for killing a girl escapes from the lockup and unwittingly pals up with the girl's real murderer. Then the cowboy learns the truth about his buddy. There's some good action in this early Wayne outing, and the star is ably supported by a number of seasoned cowboy performers. (Sony's tapes are available in Beta Hi-Fi and VHS Hi-Fi.)

SAN FERNANDO VALLEY (1944) B/W. *Dir.:* John English. *With:* Roy Rogers, Dale Evans, Jean Porter, Andrew Tombes, Bob Nolan, Vernon and Draper. **74 mins.** No rating. Beta, VHS **($24.95).** Discount. ★★★

Dale takes a back seat here, romantically speaking at least, as Rogers gets his first screen kiss from Porter. The real business the star is engaged in is bringing order to a lawless valley. The Sons of the Pioneers offer easy listening, making this an enjoyable combination of action and music.

SANTA FE SADDLEMATES. See CALLING WILD BILL ELLIOTT/ SANTA FE SADDLEMATES.

SANTA FE TRAIL (1940) B/W. *Dir.:* Michael Curtiz. *With:* Errol Flynn, Olivia de Havilland, Raymond Massey, Ronald Reagan, Van Heflin. **110 mins.** No rating. Beta, VHS **($19.95).** Crown, Kartes, Nostalgia Merchant, Prism. ★★

An uneven film that makes uncomfortable viewing. Jeb Stuart (Flynn) and George Armstrong Custer (Reagan) compete for the same woman, but share a desire to see fanatic John Brown dangling from the end of a rope. Massey's satanic interpretation of the martyred abolitionist appears to be influenced by John Barrymore's Svengali and Lionel Barrymore's Rasputin, and it's out of place in this antebellum actioner. De Havilland is the film's only undisturbing feature, probably because she's required to do nothing more than provide a beautiful contrast.

SEARCHERS, THE (1956) C. *Dir.:* John Ford. *With:* John Wayne, Jeffrey Hunter, Vera Miles, Ward Bond, Natalie Wood. **119 mins.** No rating. Beta, VHS **($59.95);** CED **($19.98).** Warner. ★★★★

This psychological western saga follows the lengthy, obsessive search of Civil War veteran Wayne for his niece, the only survivor of her slaughtered family, who has been abducted by Comanches. But he doesn't want to rescue her; he intends to kill her—a white girl contaminated by red men. Wayne is accompanied by orphaned half-breed Hunter, who was taken in by the girl's family and intends to protect her. A deeply moving film, darker and more complex than most westerns. Wayne's performance as the defeated Confederate loner with nowhere to go but on his search is magnificent.

SHANE (1953) C. *Dir.:* George Stevens. *With:* Alan Ladd, Jean Arthur, Van Heflin, Brandon de Wilde, Jack Palance. **117 mins.** No rating. Beta, VHS **($19.95);** Laser **($29.95);** CED **($19.98).** Paramount. ★★★★

A classic western about the arrival of a heroic and handsome gunfighter who helps defenseless homesteaders during the Wyoming cattle wars; the story is seen through the eyes of an impressionable child (de Wilde). Ladd's stoic face and low-key performance make him the perfect western hero, and the entire cast is first-rate, especially Palance as the mercenary villain, and de Wilde as the hero-worshipping boy. This self-conscious western realizes the mythic status of the American West, and emotionally idealizes its basic story of a stranger who rides into town, establishes law and order, and then moves on. A rich, rewarding film that is enhanced by its Oscar-winning cinematography.

SHERIFF OF CIMARRON (1945) B/W. *Dir.:* Yakima Canutt. *With:* Sunset Carson, Linda Stirling, Olin Howlin, Riley Hill, Jack Kirk, Jack Ingram, Jack O'Shea. **55 mins.** No rating. Beta, VHS **($N/A).** Nostalgia Merchant. ★★★½

Sheriff of Cimarron

One of the best and most exciting of all Carson's westerns for Republic. It's directed by stunt great Yakima Canutt with serial queen Stirling as leading lady. Don't miss it—you can rely on Canutt for fast action. Canutt wore a number of different hats in the course of his career in movies, starting with stunts and bit parts in the twenties. By 1924 he was a cowboy star, performing all his own stunts in fast-paced actioners typically released by small independent companies (which didn't do much for Canutt's visibility). His voice didn't register well in talkies, so Canutt returned to stunt work and then moved on to become a second-unit director—and a very good one. He directed some of the most stunning action sequences to come out of Hollywood. In 1966 he received a special Academy Award "for creating the profession of stuntman as it exists today and for the development of many safety devices used by stuntmen everywhere."

SHE WORE A YELLOW RIBBON (1949) C. *Dir.:* John Ford. *With:* John Wayne, Joanne Dru, John Agar, Ben Johnson. **103 mins.** No rating. Beta, VHS **($29.95)**; CED **($19.98).** Nostalgia Merchant. ★★★★

The second of Ford's trilogy of cavalry westerns—coming between *Fort Apache* and *Rio Grande*—features Wayne as an army officer whose retirement plans are postponed by an Indian attack. Ford's stock company of players offer outstanding support, and the whole effort is complemented by fantastic, Oscar-winning photography. (The film is also available from VidAmerica for $34.95, or in a "John Wayne Gift Pack" with *Flying Leathernecks* and *Fort Apache* from VidAmerica for $99.00.)

SHOOTING, THE (1966) C. *Dir.:* Monte Hellman. *With:* Jack Nicholson, Millie Perkins, Warren Oates, Will Hutchins. **82 mins.** No rating. Beta, VHS **($39.95).** Continental. ★★

There are some good moments in this obscure and confusing film, but so much is left to the imagination that the viewer's final emotion is likely to be one of frustration rather than challenge. It's never revealed just who the lead character, played by Perkins, is seeking revenge against. Perkins' character persuades two drifters (Oates and Hutchins) to join her on her unexplained quest, in the course of which they're joined by gunfighter Nicholson, with destructive results. If you see it, be willing to put some effort into trying to figure it all out.

SHOOTIST, THE (1976) C. *Dir.:* Don Siegel. *With:* John Wayne, Lauren Bacall, James Stewart, Ron Howard, Richard Boone, Sheree North, Hugh O'Brian, John Carradine, Scatman Crothers, Harry Morgan. **100 mins.** Rated PG. Beta, VHS **($59.95);** Laser **($29.95);** CED **($19.98).** Paramount. ★★★½

This low-key drama has a top-of-the-line cast involved in the tale of aging gunman J. B. Books (Wayne), whose discovery that he is dying of cancer prompts him to take a new and more compassionate view of his fellow man. Books also decides not to settle for a slow death but to die the way he has lived—with his boots on and his guns blazing. To this end he challenges three old enemies, the top gunmen of the time, to a shoot-out. This was Wayne's last movie, and one he could

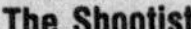

The Shootist

Silent Conflict

be proud of, although it's slow and some viewers may find it lacking in depth. The acting is every bit as impressive as you'd expect from such a terrific cast.

SILENT CONFLICT (1948) B/W. *Dir.:* George Archainbaud. *With:* Hopalong Cassidy (William Boyd), Rand Brooks. **60 mins.** No rating. Beta, VHS **($39.95).** Buena Vista. ★★½

Hopalong's friendship with Lucky (Brooks) is threatened when Lucky falls under the mysterious spell of an evil medicine man. Lucky is hypnotized to perform acts he would not ordinarily do. He even tries to murder Hoppy! Worth seeing as Hoppy's features generally had better production values and better acting than most B-westerns.

SILVER CITY KID (1944) B/W. *Dir.:* John English. *With:* Allan Lane, Peggy Stewart, Wally Vernon, Twinkle Watts, Lane Chandler, Tom Steele, Bud Geary, Jack Kirk. **55 mins.** No rating. Beta, VHS **($29.95).** Discount. ★★½

A foreman exposes gold thieves and uncovers a mining racket in this above-average offering from Republic. The star is Allan Lane in his pre-"Rocky" days. He gets adequate backing from Vernon and leading lady Stewart. You also get to meet child star Twinkle Watts.

SILVER LODE (1954) C. *Dir.:* Allan Dwan. *With:* John Payne, Lizabeth Scott, Dan Duryea, Dolores Moran, Hugh Sanders, Harry Carey, Jr., Frank Sully. **80 mins.** No rating. Beta, VHS **($59.95).** Buena Vista. ★★½

Payne's impending marriage to Scott is halted when Payne is falsely accused of murder by U.S. Marshal Duryea. The whole town shuns Payne and he must work to save his reputation and even his life. Because of the era in which it was released, anti-McCarthyism messages can easily be found. Otherwise, the action and the script are fairly routine.

SILVER SPURS (1943) B/W. *Dir.:* Joseph Kane. *With:* Roy Rogers, Jerome Cowan, John Carradine. **60 mins.** No rating. Beta, VHS **($N/A).** Video Connection. ★★★½

Here's a good one from Rogers. The plot covers a lot of territory—oil claims, mail order brides, and general crookery, but the best parts come in the latter half of the movie, which is packed with spectacular stunts by super-stuntman Canutt.

An actioner that really lives up to the name, it's a must—not just for Rogers' fans but for all western buffs. There's good work from the supporting cast.

SINISTER JOURNEY (1948) B/W. *Dir.:* George Archainbaud. *With:* Hopalong Cassidy (William Boyd), Andy Clyde, Rand Brooks. **58 mins.** No rating. Beta, VHS **($39.95).** Buena Vista. ★★½

Hopalong and his two friends Clyde and Brooks help an old friend who is threatened by a number of mysterious accidents. Blackmail and murder ensue. One of the later Hopalong features produced by Hoppy himself (William Boyd).

Sinister Journey

SIOUX CITY SUE (1946) B/W. *Dir.:* Frank McDonald. *With:* Gene Autry, Lynne Roberts, Sterling Holloway, Richard Lane, Helen Wallace, Cass County Boys. **68 mins.** No rating. Beta, VHS **($34.98).** Blackhawk. ★★★½

Don't be turned off by the cutesy title. This film is a lot of fun. Talent scouts from Paragon Pictures are searching for a singing cowboy and they come upon Autry (who else?) who has fallen on hard times. He's having to sell off his herd to make ends meet and is threatened with the loss of his homestead. The lady talent scout talks Autry into a movie (he says he'll do it if his horse gets to come along too), the proceeds of which will pay off his debts and let him keep the ranch. The cowboy finds, though, that stardom isn't quite what he expected—he winds up as a voice in a donkey cartoon. The very amusing and unusual story combines comedy with great action against a film studio background. Fine offbeat western entertainment.

SOMBRERO KID, THE (1942) B/W. *Dir.:* George Sherman. *With:* Don "Red" Barry, Lynn Merrick, Robert Homans, Joel Friedkin, Bob McKenzie. **54 mins.** No rating. Beta, VHS **($29.95).** Video Dimensions. ★★½

Our hero is accused of murdering the marshal who adopted him and must convince the townsfolk (and the law) that he did no such dastardly thing. A typically slick Republic western, but good entertainment for buffs of B-movies in general and Barry in particular. Barry was a former high-school football star who tried his hand at advertising before turning to acting. He made his first film in 1936, but nobody much cared until he starred in the serial *The Adventures of Red Ryder* in 1940. For several years Barry was listed among the top ten moneymaking western stars. Later in his career he appeared in character roles in nonwestern movies.

SONG OF ARIZONA (1946) B/W. *Dir.:* Frank McDonald. *With:* Roy Rogers, George "Gabby" Hayes, Dale Evans, Bob Nolan and the Sons of the Pioneers, Lyle Talbot. **54 mins.** No rating. Beta, VHS **($N/A).** Video Connections. ★★★

Rogers, in noble form as usual, foils a banker's plot to foreclose on a home for orphans. This is one of Rogers' better films, with good songs and plenty of action to keep the fans happy. The supporting cast of regulars does well. Solid entertainment with few disappointments.

SONG OF NEVADA (1944) B/W. *Dir.:* Joseph Kane. *With:* Roy Rogers, Dale Evans, Mary Lee, Lloyd Corrigan, Forrest Taylor. **60 mins.** No rating. Beta, VHS **($24.95).** Discount. ★★½

This is a pleasant enough tale with an extra touch of female interest—Evans almost marries the wrong man. Otherwise it's a formula Rogers vehicle with the expected mix of music and action. Not bad, but not one of the team's best.

SONG OF OLD WYOMING (1945) C. *Dir.:* Robert Emmett (Tansey). *With:* Eddie Dean, Jennifer Holt, Sarah Padden, Al "Lash" LaRue, Emmett Lynn. **65 mins.** No rating. Beta, VHS **($29.95).** Discount. ★★½

This minor Cinecolor western from the small independent PRC was the first in a series of movies to star singer Dean, who had a pleasant voice but was never an action man. This routine western has a couple of interesting cast touches. Jennifer Holt, sister of cowboy Tim, is the female interest—she appeared in a string of PRC cheapies after being dropped by Universal. LaRue made quite an impression here as the bad guy (dressed in black, he gets wiped out in the final shooting match), and this was the film that launched him on his brief and unspectacular career in the lowest of low-budget flicks.

SONG OF TEXAS (1943) B/W. *Dir.:* Joseph Kane. *With:* Roy Rogers, Harry Shannon, Pat Brady, Barton MacLane, Bob Nolan. **54 mins.** No rating. Beta, VHS **($39.95).** Video Yesteryear. ★★★

A thrilling wagon race forms the climax of this early Rogers offering, making good use of the budget, which was slightly bigger than usual for Roy's early oaters. A good story and a strong cast make this worthwhile viewing and it's one of the more durable of Rogers' films. Enough excitement to keep you on the edge of your saddle.

SONG OF THE GRINGO (1936) B/W. *Dir.:* John P. McCarthy. *With:* Tex Ritter, Joan Woodbury, Fuzzy Knight, Monte Blue, Murdock McQuarrie. **55 mins.** No rating. Beta, VHS **($24.95).** Discount. ★★

Singing cowboy Ritter rounds up the claim jumpers in this passable offering. Compared with Gene Autry's films, Ritter's were crudely made. All the same, Ritter had a good voice and handled action well, and this movie was designed to play up both talents. Real-life ex-train robber Al Jennings has a role here (in fact, during shooting he helped Ritter improve his handling of a gun). Not bad stuff.

SONG OF THE TRAIL (1936) B/W. *Dir.:* Russell Hopton. *With:* Kermit Maynard, Evelyn Brent, Fuzzy Knight, George Hayes, Bob McKenzie. **65 mins.** No rating. Beta, VHS **($29.95).** Video Dimensions. ★★½

One of Kermit Maynard's best movies with plenty of the rip-roaring action and stunts he is famous for, even though he never matched the box office popularity of his brother Ken. Antoinette Leeds (later Andrea Leeds) mades a delightful leading lady, and Knight and silent star Brent give strong support.

SON OF GOD'S COUNTRY (1948) B/W. *Dir.:* R.G. Springsteen. *With:* Monte Hale, Pamela Blake, Paul Hurst, Jim Nolan, Jason Robards, Sr., Fred Graham. **60 mins.** No rating. Beta, VHS **($29.95).** Discount. ★★

A brave marshal pretends to be a crook in order to infiltrate a gang of outlaws. A routine Republic western with a so-so role for Hale, by now promoted from supporting roles in the Sunset Carson movies to star status. Okay for undemanding viewers. Watch for former stage and silent movie star Jason Robards, Sr., who turned from young hero roles to heavies when sound came in. His son, Jason Jr., followed Dad's path to Hollywood with significant success.

SONS OF KATIE ELDER, THE (1965) C. *Dir.:* Henry Hathaway. *With:* John Wayne, Dean Martin, Earl Holliman, Michael Anderson, Jr., Martha Hyer, George Kennedy, James Gregory, Dennis Hopper. **122 mins.** No rating. Beta, VHS **($49.95);** CED **($19.98).** Paramount. ★★★

This was Wayne's first movie after his operation to remove a cancerous lung, and it's a favorite with the star's fans. A frontier woman's rowdy sons (gunfighter Wayne, gambler Martin, quiet guy Holliman, and would-be respectable citizen Anderson, Jr.) reunite to bring to justice the bad guys who killed their father and swindled their late mother out of her homestead. The real villains (Gregory and Hopper) try to frame the brothers. It's a boisterous tale, offering action and comedy in a combination that should please most western movie lovers (although Martin is always a liability in outdoor films).

SONS OF THE PIONEERS. See SUSANNA PASS/SONS OF THE PIONEERS.

SOUTH OF THE BORDER (1939) B/W. *Dir.:* George Sherman. *With:* Gene Autry, Smiley Burnette, Lupita Tobar, Duncan Renaldo. **70 mins.** No rating. Beta, VHS **($34.98).** Blackhawk. ★★★½

This is reported to be one of Autry's own favorites, and it's certainly a must for his fans. Autry and sidekick Frog go off to investigate a threat to the Latin American country of Palermo and are persuaded to help a wealthy Mexican put down the revolution. The story is based on the famous title song. Watch Autry persuade fearful caballeros to go on a cattle drive by singing to them. It's a moving and effective production with all the ingredients that make for satisfying western entertainment. Juvenile star Mary Lee made her debut here.

SPOILERS, THE (1942) B/W. *Dir.:* Ray Enright. *With:* Marlene Dietrich, John Wayne, Randolph Scott, Margaret Lindsay. **84 mins.** No rating. Beta, VHS **($39.95).** MCA. ★★★★

Here's the best of five film versions—two silent, three talking—of Rex Beach's famous story about gold miners in the Yukon. Wayne is Glennister, a miner trying to hold on to his claim and his girl, saloon owner Cherry (Dietrich), despite the machinations of gold commissioner McNamara (Scott, in a rare villainous role). Their conflict climaxes in what may be the most magnificent fight scene ever put on film. Look out for a fine performance (in his last movie) from Richard Barthelmess as Cherry's loyal partner. Another cast note: William Farnum, who starred in the 1914 original, has a supporting role as a lawyer in this version. Dietrich came into this film still riding high after her 1939 success in *Destry Rides Again* (see review), on the strength of which the role of Cherry was expanded for her and she was given top billing over her male leads.

SPRINGTIME IN THE ROCKIES (1937) B/W. *Dir.:* Joseph Kane. *With:* Gene Autry, Polly Rowles, Smiley Burnette. **60 mins.** No rating. Beta, VHS **($24.95).** Discount. ★★

An okay but unexceptional oater. This is not one of those Autry movies that the star sanctioned for release on tape through Blackhawk, who got to use Autry's own high-quality prints. Some of the unauthorized Autry films on the market are of inferior quality, so check out the print before you buy.

SPRINGTIME IN THE ROCKIES (1947) C. *Dir.:* William Witney. *With:* Roy Rogers, Andy Devine, Jane Frazee, Chester Conklin, Bob Nolan. **74 mins.** No rating. Beta, VHS **($49.95).** Video Yesteryear. ★★★½

Somewhere in the Sierra Mountains, someone is killing protected wildlife and selling the meat for an enormous profit. When a concerned old man tries to save the animals, he, too, is killed. Rogers and his cronies follow the trail of the bad guys, who are led by a woman; but it leads Roy to a chilling brush with death when he finds himself locked in a refrigeration room, surrounded by sides of beef. Fast and furious action make this one of Rogers' best films and a must for his fans.

STAGECOACH (1939) B/W. *Dir.:* John Ford. *With:* John Wayne, Claire Trevor, Thomas Mitchell, George Bancroft, John Carradine. **100 mins.** No rating. Beta, VHS **($69.95);** CED **($19.98).** Vestron. ★★★★

The greatest of traditional westerns, this John Ford classic assembles a coachful of assorted personalities, presents their somewhat adverse reactions to one another, then shows how they pull together to protect their collective skins from an Indian raid. This was by no means Wayne's first movie, although it's the one he made his mark in; he found his niche in films with his role as the earnest gunslinger the Ringo Kid. Carradine, Mitchell, and Trevor also stand out. Great performances, a taut and well-written script, the beautiful scenery of Monument Valley, Ford's loving, restrained direction, several exciting fight scenes—what more do you want from a western?

Stagecoach

STAGECOACH TO DENVER (1946) B/W. *Dir.:* R.G. Springsteen. *With:* Allan "Rocky" Lane, Bobby Blake, Martha Wentworth, Peggy Stewart, Roy Barcroft, Emmett Lynn. **56 mins.** No rating. Beta, VHS **($N/A).** Video Connection. ★★

One of the "Red Ryder" series featuring Lane as Ryder, a role he took over from Bill Elliott. Though Lane gained his only major recognition during the two years he starred as Red Ryder, it was Elliott who made the series famous and who is most identified with the role. Young Bobby Blake (Robert Blake of *Baretta)* plays Red's sidekick in the series. Below-average B-western.

STAGE TO CHINO. See DON AMIGO/STAGE TO CHINO.

STAR PACKER, THE (1934) B/W. *Dir.:* Robert N. Bradbury. *With:* John Wayne, Verna Hillie, Yakima Canutt, George "Gabby" Hayes, Earl Dwire. **53 mins.** No rating. Beta, VHS **($19.95).** Kartes, Sony, Spotlite. ★★½

An entire town is terrorized by the Shadow, the terror of the Old West, and his gang. Marshal Wayne is assigned the task of routing out the baddies and restoring law and order. The problem is he can't take on the Shadow's gang alone, and the townspeople are so scared that they're hesitant to help him. Wayne has to persuade the locals to join him in making a stand against the criminals. It's an exciting, fast-paced adventure for Wayne, with lots of action and a strong supporting cast. (Sony's tapes are available in Beta Hi-Fi and VHS Hi-Fi.)

STATION WEST (1948) B/W. *Dir.:* Sidney Lanfield. *With:* Dick Powell, Jane Greer, Agnes Moorehead, Burl Ives, Raymond Burr. **92 mins.** No rating. Beta, VHS **($34.98).** Blackhawk. ★★★

Army officer Powell goes undercover to flush out the

Station West

perpetrators of a series of gold thefts. Powell, in a rare western role, heads a fine cast that ably backs up his own solid performance. Western fans may wish he'd made more movies in the genre since he looks so good in this one. Solid entertainment.

STORM OVER WYOMING. See RIDERS OF THE RANGE/STORM OVER WYOMING.

STRANGER AND THE GUNFIGHTER, THE (1976) C. *Dir.:* Anthony Dawson. *With:* Lee Van Cleef, Lo Lieh, Karen Yeh. **106 mins.** Rated PG. Beta, VHS **($59.95).** RCA/Columbia. ★★

This is a strange mix—a western with kung fu overtones in a period setting. It's one of a spate of foreign-made action and violence films that followed the Clint Eastwood spaghetti western successes. Here squint-eyed Dakota (Van Cleef) accidentally kills a wealthy Chinese lord in the course of an attempted robbery. He's after the loot, but finds only clues to the rich man's fortune. The dead man's family dispatch one of their number to hunt down Dakota and restore the family's honor. The chosen one is the dead man's nephew Ho Kiang (Lo Lieh), a kung fu expert. When Ho catches up with Dakota, the latter convinces him that the killing was indeed accidental, and the two team up in seach of the missing fortune. Seems that the crucial clues to the whereabouts of the fortune are in the possession of the dead man's four mistresses—*very* close possession, in fact, since the clues are tatooed on the ladies' rear ends. A further complication arises when the fourth mistress (Karen Yeh), with whom Ho has fallen in love, is kidnapped by a rival gang. With her, of course, goes the final clue. Dakota and Ho now have to confront the other gang and rescue the lady. This odd compromise between several different movie genres has its moments, but it's strictly for tolerant viewers.

SUDDEN DEATH. See GUNFIRE/SUDDEN DEATH.

SUNDOWN KID (1942) B/W. *Dir.:* Elmer Clifton. *With:* Don Barry, Ian Keith, Helen Mackeller, Linda Johnson, Emmett Lynn. **57 mins.** No rating. Beta, VHS **($29.95).** Discount. ★★½

An intrepid girl reporter exposes counterfeiters in this okay effort. Republic's Don "Red" Barry westerns were small-scale but well produced and usually action-packed. This one is a good bet for fans of the star, and there's a solid performance from Keith as the heavy.

SUNSET IN EL DORADO (1945) B/W. *Dir.:* Frank McDonald. *With:* Roy Rogers, Dale Evans, George "Gabby" Hayes, Margaret Dumont, Roy Barcroft. **56 mins.** No rating. Beta, VHS **($N/A).** Video Connections. ★★

Here's a story within a story. Evans visits a ghost town and in a dream sequence becomes her own grandmother, the notorious dancehall queen Kansas Kate. In fact, all the film's modern characters are transposed into the lost days of the ghost town. Quite an intriguing tale for a western. The cast includes Marx Brothers funny lady Margaret Dumont. The Sons of the Pioneers are in good voice.

SUNSET TRAIL, THE (1932) B/W. *Dir.:* Breezy Reeves Eason. *With:* Ken Maynard, Ruth Hiatt, Philo McCullough, Frank Rice, Buddy Hunter, Slim Whitaker. **62 mins.** No rating. Beta, VHS **($24.95).** Discount. ★★

This Maynard outing marked the second appearance of Rice as the star's sidekick. The two had appeared in *The Fighting Legion*, and Maynard found the partnership so comfortable that he chose Rice to partner him in this one, too. The two were to team up again for a number of features in Maynard's second series for Universal in 1933-34. Rice was familiar with the plot of *The Sunset Trail.* The same story had been filmed as *Shadow Ranch* in 1930 and Rice had even played the same role, except opposite Buck Jones.

SUPPORT YOUR LOCAL SHERIFF (1969) C. *Dir.:* Burt Kennedy. *With:* James Garner, Joan Hackett, Walter Brennan, Harry Morgan, Jack Elam, Bruce Dern. **93 mins.** Rated G. Beta, VHS **($59.95);** CED **($19.98).** Key. ® ★★★½

This terrific comedy-western treats audiences to the best of both worlds. Townspeople accidentally come across gold (the precious stuff surfaces while they're digging a grave), and the town is infected by gold rush fever—and the attendant scams perpetrated by local baddies who want to get rich quick. Ruffian Pa Darby (Brennan) is one of the crooked schemers. He decides to levy a tax on all gold carried through his property, which conveniently includes the road into town. Seeking a sheriff to put a stop to this lawlessness, the townsfolk recruit adventurer James McCullough (Garner) who's just passing through on his way to Australia. Having other plans, McCullough doesn't much want the job, but he stays on anyway. Great casting helps make this an all-around winner. It's fun, and it's funny. See it.

SUSANNA PASS/SONS OF THE PIONEERS (1949/1942) C/B&W. *Dir.:* William Witney/Joseph Kane. *With:* Roy Rogers, Dale Evans, Estelita Rodriguez/Roy Rogers, George "Gabby" Hayes, Maris Wrixon, Forrest Taylor. **121 mins.** No rating. Beta, VHS **($39.95).** Republic. ★★★/★

Here are two Rogers movies made seven years apart, and the later one is definitely the better. *Susanna Pass* is a satisfying actioner with our heroes standing up to crooks who are trying to block the pass. Evans and Rodriguez brighten up the picture, and there's some good stunt work from David Sharpe. Pleasant songs, too, from Foy Willing and the Riders of the Purple Sage.

Sons of the Pioneers, on the other hand, has little to offer any but the most devoted of Rogers' fans. It's slow and short on action or entertainment value. Too bad no one thought to choose a better movie and make this a really pleasing double bill.

TALL IN THE SADDLE (1944) B/W. *Dir.:* Edwin L. Marin. *With:* John Wayne, Ella Raines, George "Gabby" Hayes, Raymond Hatton, Ward Bond. **79 mins.** No rating. Beta, VHS **($29.95).** Nostalgia Merchant. ★★★

Dated but satisfactory A-western from RKO with a fine cast. Wayne stars as a cowhand who can find nothing good to say about women. When a high-spirited woman (Raines) and her daughter take over the ranch where the Duke is the foreman, he finds that he has met his match. The plot may be predictable, but Wayne and Raines are quite enjoyable, while the supporting cast boasts a fine ensemble of veteran western actors (Hayes, Hatton, and Bond).

TELL THEM WILLIE BOY IS HERE (1969) C. *Dir.:* Abraham Polonsky. *With:* Robert Redford, Katharine Ross, Robert Blake, Susan Clark, Barry Sullivan. **98 mins.** Rated PG. Beta, VHS **($39.95).** MCA. ★★½

A disappointing film that doesn't deliver nearly as much as

it purports to offer. The anti-discrimination theme—the Indian as the victim of injustice—was very popular at the time this film was made, and the director had personal experience with the subject because he'd been a victim of the McCarthy witch-hunts. Despite this potentially fruitful combination, however, the film doesn't jell. Even a very strong cast, including then star-on-the-rise Redford, can't overcome the disadvantages of stereotypical characterization and an inappropriate slickness that spreads a pall of superficiality over the theme. The Willie Boy of the title is a young Paiute Indian, played by Blake, who accidentally kills the father of his girlfriend (Ross) and, with the girl, goes on the run. Assistant sheriff Cooper (Redford) is supposed to go after the fleeing lovers, even though his heart isn't in the chase. When Willie accidentally shoots one of the posse, Cooper is forced to go after him for real. The film is based on Harry Lawton's novel *Willie Boy.*

TENNESSEE'S PARTNER (1955) C. *Dir.:* Allan Dwan. *With:* John Payne, Ronald Reagan, Rhonda Fleming, Coleen Gray. **87 mins.** No rating. Beta, VHS **($59.95).** Buena Vista. ★★½

A good-hearted gold miner called Cowpoke (Reagan) sides with a hard-drinking, hard-living gambler named Tennessee (Payne) in a quarrel. Then the two are accused of murdering an elderly prospector. How do they get out of this one? Fleming plays "The Duchess," the fiery-headed woman who runs the saloon where much of the action takes place. This screen translation of Bret Harte's story makes a fairly interesting western and gives Reagan what is considered one of his best roles.

TEXAS GUN-FIGHTER (1932) B/W. *Dir.:* Phil Rosen. *With:* Ken Maynard, Sheila Manners, Harry Woods, James Mason, Bob Fleming, Roy Bucko, Buck Bucko. **63 mins.** No rating. Beta, VHS **($24.95).** Discount. ★★

An outlaw thwarts a villain's attempt to abduct a girl during a stagecoach holdup and finds he's undertaken to get her to safety—which turns out to be a far from easy task. This is a rehash of *The Lone Rider*, the 1930 Buck Jones release that was Jones' first talking picture. This time around Maynard has the Jones role and Woods repeats the role of the villain he played in the earlier version. The James Mason listed in the cast is not the well-known British actor of the same name.

Texas Gun-fighter was released by a minor production company called Tiffany Pictures.

TEXAS JUSTICE (1942) B/W. *Dir.:* Sam Newfield. *With:* George Houston, Al "Fuzzy" St. John, Dennis Moore, Wanda McKay, Claire Rochelle, Slim Whitaker. **58 mins.** No rating. Beta, VHS **($24.95).** Discount. ★★

This is a routine tale from the "Lone Rider" series that PRC put out with Houston in the lead (Robert Livingston later took over as star). Houston was an unlikely candidate for western stardom. He graduated from Rutgers and Juilliard, and sang with the American Opera Company and on Broadway before making his first screen appearance in 1935. He was cast in musicals and dramas before making a sudden switch, adopting a new persona as the Lone Rider, and joining the ranks of cowboy heroes.

TEXAS TERROR (1940) B/W. *Dir.:* Robert N. Bradbury. *With:* John Wayne, Lucile Brown, LeRoy Mason, George "Gabby" Hayes, Buffalo Bill, Jr., Yakima Canutt. **50 mins.** No rating. Beta Hi-Fi, VHS Hi-Fi **($19.95).** Sony. ★★½

In pursuit of a band of outlaws, cowboy Wayne kills his best friend—at least he believes that he was responsible. Ashamed and sick at heart, he retreats from society and retires to the solitary life of a prospector in the desert. The dead man's sister returns to town, but Wayne can't face her. However, she holds the clue that will lead him to his friend's real killer. Wayne gets good support from Brown, heroine of many B-westerns, and the rest of the cast. Look out for a terrific fight scene.

TEX RIDES WITH THE BOY SCOUTS (1937) B/W. *Dir.:* Ray Taylor. *With:* Tex Ritter, Marjorie Reynolds, Snub Pollard, Horace Murphy, Charles King. **60 mins.** No rating. Beta, VHS **($24.95).** Discount. ★★½

This is probably the best of the movies Ritter made for Grand National, and it offers enough action to keep the viewer's eyes on the screen. The cowboy's sidekick is played by Snub Pollard, who had been Ritter's favorite screen comedian when Ritter was younger. Learning that Pollard was down on his luck, Ritter persuaded his studio to give the comic a small part in his 1936 movie *Headin' for the Rio Grande.* The two

Tex Rides With the Boy Scouts

They Died With Their Boots On

performers went on to develop a solid screen partnership, which is clearly apparent here.

THEY CAME TO CORDURA (1959) C. *Dir.:* Robert Rossen. *With:* Gary Cooper, Rita Hayworth, Van Heflin, Tab Hunter, Richard Conte, Michael Callan, Dick York. **123 mins.** No rating. Beta, VHS **($59.95)**. RCA/Columbia. ★★★

Cooper's next-to-last movie casts him as Major Thorne, a man labeled a coward, who conducts a trek across the desert toward a military assembly point at Cordura. One of the party is a mysterious American fugitive (Hayworth). This is a good but not great movie about what courage really is. Cooper's performance is impressive. Stick with it, even if you find it slow in the beginning.

THEY DIED WITH THEIR BOOTS ON (1941) B/W. *Dir.:* Raoul Walsh. *With:* Errol Flynn, Olivia de Havilland, Arthur Kennedy, Anthony Quinn. **141 mins.** No rating. Beta, VHS **($59.98).** Key. ★★★

A star-studded film based on General George Armstrong Custer's infamous last stand at Little Bighorn. Although it's not historically accurate, it's never dull, and Flynn plays Custer with just the right touch of foreboding. The scene in which he says good-bye to his faithful wife, Libby (de Havilland), is made doubly poignant by the fact that this was the famous screen team's last film together. Anthony Quinn plays Sioux chief Crazy Horse, and the fine supporting cast also includes Sydney Greenstreet, Hattie McDaniel, Charley Grapewin, and Gene Lockhart.

THREE FACES WEST (1940) B/W. *Dir.:* Bernard Vorhaus. *With:* John Wayne, Sigrid Gurie, Charles Coburn. **79 mins.** No rating. Beta, VHS **($39.95).** Republic. ★★½

This minor Wayne vehicle casts him as a cowboy guiding a group of refugees who are in flight from the Nazis during World War II. The story hinges on an Austrian doctor, one of the refugees, who attempts with the support of the townspeople to practice in dust bowl territory. This is a sincere and well-played drama in a western setting, rather than a regular western. Good for fans who like something a bit different.

THREE MESQUITEERS, THE (1936) B/W. *Dir.:* Ray Taylor. *With:* Bob Livingston, Ray Corrigan, Syd Saylor, Kay Hughes, J.P. McGowan, Frank Yaconelli. **61 mins.** No rating. Beta, VHS **($N/A).** Video Connection. ★★

The first of the "Three Mesquiteers" series, with Livingston as Stony Brooke, Corrigan as Tucson Smith, and Saylor as Lullaby Joslin. It's a story about veterans who settle in the west after World War I but find their lives complicated by warfare of a different kind in the form of harassment by villain McGowan and his gang of cattle thieves. After this movie Saylor was replaced as Lullaby by Max Terhune.

THUNDERING HERD, THE. See BUFFALO STAMPEDE.

THUNDER IN GOD'S COUNTRY (1951) B/W. *Dir.:* George Blair. *With:* Rex Allen, Mary Ellen Kay, Buddy Ebsen, Ian McDonald, Paul Harvey. **67 mins.** No rating. Beta, VHS **($29.95).** Discount. ★★½

An escaped convict threatens townspeople in this enjoyable Rex Allen western from Republic. Allen, brought in to replace Monte Hale, was the last western player Republic put any work into promoting. He made 31 pictures for them beginning with *The Arizona Cowboy* in 1949. This is a passable example of his work, and there are good performances from heroine Kay and sidekick Ebsen.

THUNDER IN THE DESERT (1937) B/W. *Dir.:* Sam Newfield. *With:* Bob Steele, Louise Stanley, Don Barclay, Charles King, Ed Brady. **60 mins.** No rating. Beta, VHS **($24.95).** Discount. ★★

Popular cowboy star Steele stars in this western tale typical of most of Steele's films. Often featured as one of the "Three

Mesquiteers," here he goes it alone in this action-oriented adventure.

THUNDER TRAIL (1937) B/W. *Dir.:* Charles T. Barton. *With:* Gilbert Roland, Marsha Hunt, Charles Bickford, J. Carrol Naish, James Craig, Monte Blue. **58 mins.** No rating. Beta, VHS **($24.95).** Discount. ★★★

Two brothers survive an outlaw raid. The experience has a different effect on each brother—one becomes an outlaw, the other a force for law and order. The plot is far from fresh, but all the same, the competent cast and good production values serve the familiar story well in this okay actioner based on Zane Grey's *Arizona Ames.* Latin heartbreaker Roland is in fine form. Note that you may find this film incorrectly listed in some catalogs as *Thunder Pass.*

TOMBSTONE CANYON (1932) B/W. *Dir.:* Alan James. *With:* Ken Maynard, Sheldon Lewis, Cecilia Parker, Lafe McKee. **60 mins.** No rating. Beta, VHS **($24.98).** Discount. ★★½

A silly tale about a crazy killer, known as the Phantom (Lewis), who wears a mask to hide a facial disfigurement and goes around emitting weird screams and terrorizing the locals. Eventually hero Maynard discovers that the Phantom is really his long-lost father. A likely story! But it's passable fun. This was leading lady Parker's first film opposite Maynard.

TOM HORN (1980) C. *Dir.:* William Wiard. *With:* Steve McQueen, Linda Evans, Richard Farnsworth, Billy Green Bush, Slim Pickens. **98 mins.** Rated R. Beta, VHS **($64.95).** Warner. ★★½

Disappointing version of what should have been a good film about the last days of gunman Tom Horn, played by McQueen. There were strong story possibilities in the real-life Horn's letters from jail claiming that he'd been framed for the murder for which he'd been convicted, but the filmmakers failed to make use of them. Moreover the succession of different screenwriters and directors who worked on the movie is evident in the prevailing confusion that mars the final product. McQueen's study of Tom Horn (this was the actor's last film but one) has some good moments, but the film's strong point is its magnificent photography, the work of John Alonzo. The original plan was to base the movie not on Horn's own autobiography but on Will Henry's novel, *I, Tom Horn*. It might have been better for everyone if they'd stuck to that plan.

TONTO KID, THE (1935) B/W. *Dir.:* Robert N. Bradbury. *With:* Rex Bell, Ruth Mix, Buzz Barton, Theodore Lorch, Barbara Roberts, Murdock McQuarrie, Stella Adams. **60 mins.** No rating. Beta, VHS **($24.95).** Discount. ★★

Passable entertainment from Bell, a good-looking actor who played leads and supporting roles in both silent and talking comedies and dramas before trying on his cowboy boots in the thirties. Although he'd had some success with other genres, it was in westerns that Bell really made a name—unless you count his well-publicized elopement with "It" girl Clara Bow in 1931. The two stars settled in Nevada, where Bell extended his interests to local politics. He was elected Lieutenant Governor of Nevada in 1954, and in 1958 made an unsuccessful bid for Governor.

TO THE LAST MAN (1933) B/W. *Dir.:* Henry Hathaway. *With:* Randolph Scott, Esther Ralston, Buster Crabbe, Noah Beery, Sr., Barton MacLane, Fuzzy Knight, Gail Patrick, Shirley Temple. **70 mins.** No rating. Beta, VHS **($24.95).** Discount. ★★★

A winning cast and lots of action make this one of the best of Paramount's Zane Grey westerns. It's about a bloody family feud that's finally healed by the influence of young love. Shirley Temple, then four years old, has a small part. This was a remake of a 1923 silent, and was remade in its turn in 1947 as *Thunder Mountain.*

TRAIL BEYOND, THE (1934) B/W. *Dir.:* Robert N. Bradbury. *With:* John Wayne, Noah Beery, Jr., Verna Hillie, Iris Lancaster. **57 mins.** No rating. Beta, VHS **($19.95).** Sony, Spotlite. ★★★

It's Wayne to the rescue in this exciting, stunt-filled film. Rod Drew (Wayne) and his pal Wabi (Beery, Jr.) travel to the Northwest and discover a map that will lead them to hidden gold on the upper Ombibaki River. Like any red-blooded western heroes, they go after the gold, but their attention is deflected by a damsel in distress. A young girl has been kidnapped and imprisoned by a gang of villains and it's up to Wayne to save her life and her gold mine. Hillie is a charming heroine. One of the best of the early Monogram series. (Sony's tapes are available in Beta Hi-Fi and VHS Hi-Fi.)

TRAIL DRIVE, THE (1935) B/W. *Dir.:* Alan James. *With:* Ken Maynard, Cecilia Parker, William Gould, Wally Wales. **63 mins.** No rating. Beta, VHS **($N/A).** Video Connection. ★★★

The situation looks bad for Maynard. He's locked in a closet and tied to the door. But our hero manages to get loose and throws himself, still tied to the door, over a balcony and on to the surprised horses below. This stunt alone would make this Universal western worth watching, and the rest of it is okay viewing too.

TRAIL OF ROBIN HOOD/ROMANCE ON THE RANGE (1950/1942) C/B&W. *Dir.:* William Witney/Joseph Kane. *With:* Roy Rogers, Jack Holt, Penny Edwards, Rex Allen, Monte Hall, William Farnum/Roy Rogers, George "Gabby" Hayes, Sally Payne, Linda Hayes. **120 mins.** No rating. Beta, VHS **($39.95).** Republic. ★★★★/★

Lots of charm here in one of Rogers' most delightful films. Retired cowboy star Jack Holt sells low-cost Christmas trees to the poor. When rivals try to put an end to Holt's philanthropic endeavor, Rogers and a gaggle of other Republic western stars come to his aid. This movie represented Republic's last major attempt to boost the waning popularity of the B-western. It's in color, and every cowboy on the lot was thrown into the cast—including Allan "Rocky" Lane, Ray Corrigan, Tom Tyler, Tom Keene, and Kermit Maynard. Even bad guy George Chesebro gets into the act. Terrific fun for western buffs. Don't miss it.

Do, however, miss *Romance on the Range.* The title tells you all you need to know about this inferior early Rogers flick. Again, it's a matter of throwing in a cheapie to fill up a double bill after a good come-on film. That's the breaks.

TRAIL STREET (1947) B/W. *Dir.:* Ray Enright. *With:* Randolph Scott, Robert Ryan, Anne Jeffries, George "Gabby" Hayes. **84 mins.** No rating. Beta, VHS **($34.98).** Blackhawk. ★★★

William Corcoran's novel *Golden Horizon* provides the basis for this one. Scott stars as legendary character Bat Masterson, saving the townspeople from the machinations of cattle rustlers and shady cattlemen who are trying to turn the struggling farmers off their land. Despite the well-worn plot, this is an exciting A-western, full of action and very entertaining. Anne Jeffries, who later appeared in TV's *Topper*, makes an attractive leading lady.

Trail Street

TRAIN ROBBERS, THE (1973) C. *Dir.:* Burt Kennedy. *With:* John Wayne, Ann-Margret, Rod Taylor, Ben Johnson, Christopher George, Ricardo Montalban. **92 mins.** Rated PG. Beta, VHS **($59.95).** Warner. ★★

Pity the poor cast of this inferior offering—they got robbed of time and energy that they'd have been much better advised to spend elsewhere. The story, such as it is, has Ann-Margret on the hunt for half a million dollars in gold treasure originally stolen by her late husband. Prospects of a hefty reward prompt Wayne and his buddies to help the lady. A gang of gunmen are searching for the searchers. That's about it. The actors wasted their time, but that doesn't mean you have to follow suit.

TRAITOR, THE (1936) B/W. *Dir.:* Sam Newfield. *With:* Tim McCoy, Frances Grant, Wally Wales, Karl Hackett, Jack Rockwell, Pedro Regas. **57 mins.** No rating. Beta, VHS **($24.95).** Discount. ★★

McCoy's last film for Puritan has the star posing as a disgraced Texas Ranger in order to get his man. Puritan's westerns tended to be short on action and long on psychology, and this one offers more of the same. It's interesting enough, but definitely slow. At the time *The Traitor* was released, McCoy had signed a deal with Imperial to do eight pictures at $4000 a picture, but Imperial tried to pull out of the contract and McCoy took them to court. The case was settled in his favor and he was awarded $37,000, but the contract dispute kept him off the screen for a while and McCoy, like so many other western stars, used the time to get his act together and take it on the road. Also like so many other western stars, however, he bombed. His road show was not a success and lost him many thousands of dollars.

TRIGGER JR./THE FAR FRONTIER (1950/1948) C/B&W. *Dir.:* William Witney/William Witney. *With:* Roy Rogers, Dale Evans, Pat Brady/Roy Rogers, Andy Devine, Clayton Moore, Gail Davis, Roy Barcroft. **122 mins.** No rating. Beta, VHS **($39.95).** Republic. ★★½/★★

My Pal Trigger, Rogers' first A-budget western and reputed to be his favorite film, came out in 1946, and clearly there had to be a sequel. This is it. Trigger's colt, Trigger Jr., helps Pa and Roy break up a gang of diamond smugglers. The photography is beautiful, so it's a real eyeful not only for horse lovers but for all audiences. See it.

The Far Frontier, made two years earlier than *Trigger Jr.,* is pretty routine Rogers fare. Trigger and son are a hard act to follow.

TRIGGER TRIO, THE (1937) B/W. *Dir.:* William Witney. *With:* Ralph Byrd, Ray Corrigan, Max Terhune, Sandra Corday, Hal Taliaferro (Wally Wales). **54 mins.** No rating. Beta, VHS **($N/A).** Video Connection. ★★★

A lightning-paced "Three Mesquiteers" tale with Ralph (Dick Tracy) Byrd temporarily replacing series regular Bob Livingston, who suffered a fractured skull just before shooting was due to start. The story: Foot-and-mouth disease causes panic on the ranges; authorities try to keep the dreaded outbreak in check; and Corrigan and Terhune come to the rescue. This was 20-year-old Witney's directorial debut, and it's an honorable one. Western fans will like this a lot.

TROUBLE BUSTERS (1933) B/W. *Dir.:* Lew Collins. *With:* Jack Hoxie, Lane Chandler, Kaye Edwards, Slim Whitaker, Ben Corbett, Harry Todd. **55 mins.** No rating. Beta, VHS **($24.95).** Discount. ★★

Pleasant entertainment from Hoxie, one of Universal's big names of the early twenties who, probably because the market was simply overloaded, began to lose ground in the mid-twenties. He made *Trouble Busters* for Majestic in 1933, but the best of his career was over. Hoxie was married to Marin Sais, who costarred in many of his movies.

TROUBLE IN TEXAS (1937) B/W. *Dir.:* Robert N. Bradbury. *With:* Tex Ritter, Rita Cansino (Hayworth), Earl Dwire, Yakima Canutt. **65 mins.** No rating. Beta, VHS **($24.95).** Discount. ★★½

This Ritter movie is noteworthy for the presence of Rita Cansino—later to become famous as Rita Hayworth—in the role of an undercover agent who helps the hero solve a series of rodeo robberies. Horace Murphy plays Ritter's sidekick, and top stuntman Canutt doubles for Ritter as well as having a small role of his own. The Grand National oaters lack the polish of some of the competition, but they provide reliable entertainment for B-western buffs.

TRUE GRIT (1969) C. *Dir.:* Henry Hathaway. *With:* John Wayne, Glen Campbell, Kim Darby, Robert Duvall, Jeremy Slate, Strother Martin, Jeff Corey. **128 mins.** Rated G. Beta, VHS **($66.95);** Laser **($35.95);** CED **($29.98).** Paramount. ★★★★

Wayne stars as Rooster Cogburn, a rough, tough, one-eyed marshal given to booze and cussing. For a fee, he agrees to help 14-year-old Mattie Ross (Kim Darby) in her search for her father's killer. The unlikely pair are accompanied by Texas Ranger La Boeuf (Campbell), who has his own reasons for wanting to catch the quarry. It's a rollicking good story and engrossing entertainment, especially for nostalgia buffs. Campbell is not entirely at home with his role, but Wayne's fits him as comfortably as his familiar western garb—he got an Oscar for his performance into the bargain. The movie spawned an inferior sequel, *Rooster Cogburn* (see review), in which Wayne played the title role opposite costar Katharine Hepburn.

TULSA (1949) C. *Dir.:* Stuart Heisler. *With:* Susan Hayward, Robert Preston, Pedro Armendariz, Chill Wills. **96 mins.** No rating. Beta, VHS **($N/A).** Nostalgia Merchant. ★★½

Passable western with an interesting cast. Hayward, who had already become an established Hollywood star and received acclaim (and the first of five Oscar nominations) for *Smash-up: The Story of a Woman* in 1949, plays the gutsy owner of oil-rich land who has to fight for her property with any means at hand. Her costar is Preston, who had many years of fine acting behind him before finding stardom as *The Music Man* on Broadway and then on film. The teaming of two strong performers makes this fairly ordinary tale worth watching, and the leads are backed up by a strong supporting cast.

TULSA KID, THE (1940) B/W. *Dir.:* George Sherman. *With:* Don "Red" Barry, Noah Beery, Sr., Luana Walters, David Durand. **56 mins.** No rating. Beta, VHS **($N/A).** Nostalgia Merchant. ★★½

Adequate entertainment from Don "Red" Barry, released at a time when the studios were turning out solid western fare as fast as they could manage. Here Barry plays a man confronting his outlaw foster-father, played by reliable heavy Noah Beery. Fans of the star will like this.

TUMBLEWEEDS (1925) B/W. *Dir.:* King Baggot. *With:* William S. Hart, Barbara Bedford, Lucien Littlefield, J. Gordon Russell, Richard R. Neill. **114 mins.** Silent. No rating. Beta, VHS **($49.95).** Video Yesteryear. ★★★★

The opening of the Cherokee Strip in 1889 is the background for this famous film about a girl's battle against vicious land grabbers. One of the great westerns, with perhaps the most spectacular land rush sequence ever filmed, this was silent immortal William S. Hart's last film. Hart plays Don Carver, a cattle drover for whom the end of the drives means the loss of his livelihood. With his girl, Molly (Bedford), he sets out to make a home on the Cherokee Strip. Among his adventures en route is an escape from jail—with the help of his faithful horse. A must for western buffs. This version in-

Tumbleweeds

Two Mules for Sister Sara

cludes Hart's eight-minute sound introduction, made for the film's 1939 reissue; the silent portion of the tape has a music soundtrack and is shown at correct silent projection speed.

TWO MULES FOR SISTER SARA (1970) C. *Dir.:* Don Siegel. *With:* Clint Eastwood, Shirley MacLaine, Manolo Fabregas, Alberto Morin. **105 mins.** Rated PG. Beta, VHS **($69.95).** MCA. ★★½

Drifter Eastwood prevents the rape of a naked girl and gets a big surprise when he sees her clothed—she's wearing a nun's habit. But why is she dressed as a nun when she's actually a hooker? Plenty of action and moments of charm don't add up to a satisfying movie. See it if you like the stars.

UNDER CALIFORNIA STARS (1948) C. *Dir.:* William Witney. *With:* Roy Rogers, Andy Devine, Jane Frazee, Michael Chapin, Bob Nolan and the Sons of the Pioneers. **71 mins.** No rating. Beta, VHS **($49.95).** Video Yesteryear. ★★★

An above-average Rogers western in which Roy's famous steed is snatched by wild horse rustlers. Obviously, our hero is good and mad and all attention focuses on efforts to get the palomino back. Good supporting performances from a familiar cast. The film is in color—which was unusual for a western of this period—so the California skies of the title are seen in all their splendor (and so is Trigger's beautiful hide).

UNDER WESTERN STARS (1938) B/W. *Dir.:* Joseph Kane. *With:* Roy Rogers, Smiley Burnette, Carol Hughes, Guy Usher. **54 mins.** No rating. Beta, VHS **($24.95).** Discount. ★★★½

Rogers' first starring western is a humdinger intended originally as an Autry vehicle. Unfortunately, this is an edited version and not the original 65-minute film. Rogers plays a congressman who goes to Washington to plead on behalf of inhabitants of a dustbowl area. (Autry recorded the famous song "Dust.") Rogers got the movie because at the time Autry was involved in a contract dispute with Republic—he had just finished *The Old Barn Dance* and was refusing to make any more pictures until his contract was renegotiated. One Dick Weston, who had had a singing role in *The Old Barn Dance*, was looking for work, and Republic signed him, renamed him Roy Rogers (a second name change for the actor who was born Leonard Slye), and offered him the Autry role in *Under*

Western Stars. Rogers even got Autry's sidekick Burnette as his costar. Although the studio was obviously using him to keep Autry's demands in line, Rogers recognized the importance of this boost to his career. Republic, in turn, recognized that they were on to a hot number in Rogers and rapidly stepped up his budgets and started assigning top quality moviemakers to his films.

UTAH (1945) B/W. *Dir.:* John English. *With:* Roy Rogers, Dale Evans, George "Gabby" Hayes, Peggy Stewart, Grant Withers, Bob Nolan and the Sons of the Pioneers. **54 mins.** No rating. Beta, VHS **($24.95).** Discount. ★★★

When the ranch owner dies, foreman Rogers and cowhands Hayes and the Sons of the Pioneers get a new employer—and she's a woman (Evans). She's also a musical-comedy star who's more interested in her career than her newly acquired cows, and she's all set to sell out to a crooked land broker. Rogers and co. have to dissuade her from this dastardly plan. Top-notch blend of guns, girls, and songs make this one of Rogers' best. There's a terrific finale set in the Chicago stockyards. And, yes, Evans finally sees the error of her ways. Note that this is the inferior 54-minute version of this movie, not the original 78-minute one.

Utah

UTAH TRAIL (1938) B/W. *Dir.:* Al Herman. *With:* Tex Ritter, Horace Murphy, Snub Pollard, Adele Pierce (Pamela Blake),

Dave O'Brien, Charles King, Bud Osborne. **56 mins.** No rating. Beta, VHS **($24.95).** Discount. ★★

Ritter himself came up with the idea of a story about a ghost train for this, his last flick for Grand National. Ritter took a keen interest in the plots of his movies and usually sat in on story conferences. This is an okay tale in which Ritter appears with sidekick Pollard and regular villain King. Ritter rarely used a stand-in for his screen fights, and King taught him a lot about fisticuffs for the camera. Despite their on-screen hostility, the two men enjoyed working together.

UTAH WAGON TRAIN (1951) B/W. *Dir.:* Philip Ford. *With:* Rex Allen, Penny Edwards, Buddy Ebsen, Roy Barcroft, Sarah Padden, Grant Withers. **67 mins.** No rating. Beta, VHS **($29.95).** Discount. ★★½

A rancher has to solve a murder in order to hold on to his land in this entry from the string of features Allen made for Republic (starting with *The Arizona Cowboy* in 1949). Allen projects a pleasant, unsophisticated screen persona, and this is a typically likable movie for fans of the star. The story moves along at a good pace, and the supporting cast give it their best.

VALLEY OF FIRE (1951) B/W. *Dir.:* John English. *With:* Gene Autry, Pat Buttram, Gail Davis, Russell Hayden, Christine Larsen. **63 mins.** No rating. Beta, VHS **($34.98).** Blackhawk. ★★★

This quirky story with stronger than usual female interest has Autry importing a bunch of brides as part of his campaign to civilize a frontier town. The story is set in the 1890s and Autry, as mayor of Quartz Creek, has his hands full. First he rids the town of a crooked gambler and his gambling hall hostess, then he turns his attention to the townsfolk. Deciding that some female influence might steady the rough-and-ready guys, he arranges to bring in a selection of brides. It's another offbeat story angle that makes for a thoroughly entertaining film. Davis, TV's Annie Oakley, is the female lead. Songs include "Here's to the Ladies" and "On Top of Old Smoky."

VANISHING WESTERNER, THE (1950) B/W. *Dir.:* Philip Ford. *With:* Monte Hale, Paul Hurst, Aline Towne, Roy Barcroft. **60 mins.** No rating. Beta, VHS **($29.95).** Discount. ★★

A routine outing for Hale, one of the less prominent of Republic's cowboy stars of the forties. The title, for Hale, was something of a prophecy—this movie was released about the time the studio decided to replace Hale with Rex Allen, who was the last of Republic's B-western stars. Here Hale is a U.S. marshal investigating the problems that beset a stagecoach line. Good action.

VERA CRUZ (1954) C. *Dir.:* Robert Aldrich. *With:* Gary Cooper, Burt Lancaster, Denise Darcel, Cesar Romero, George Macready, Sarita Montiel, Ernest Borgnine, Charles Bronson, Jack Elam. **94 mins.** No rating. Beta, VHS **($59.98);** CED **($19.98).** CBS/Fox. ★★★

In 1866, during the Mexican Revolution, two American adventurers (Cooper and Lancaster) become involved with a beautiful adventuress, a gold shipment, and intrigue among the rebels. Successful big-star teaming and an unusual plot twist give the film some value; it's fun to watch Cooper and Lancaster in tandem, even though there's not much plot to back up their efforts. All in all, this is a patchy effort, albeit good-looking enough to let you overlook some of the inadequacies.

Vera Cruz

VIGILANTES OF BOOM TOWN (1946) B/W. *Dir.:* R.G. Springsteen. *With:* Allan "Rocky" Lane, Bobby Blake, Roy Barcroft, Martha Wentworth, Peggy Stewart. **54 mins.** No rating. Beta, VHS **($N/A).** Nostalgia Merchant. ★★½

A superior Red Ryder tale from Republic with Lane in the lead. He's trying to prevent a bank robbery that has been planned to take place during a world championship boxing match. Lane made this one the year he replaced Bill Elliott as Red Ryder. Lane had been playing in westerns for ten years (he was Tim Holt's partner in crime in *The Law West of Tombstone* in 1937), but it was as Red Ryder that he really began to make his mark. He played the role through 1947 until Republic sold the series and began to develop "Rocky" Lane into a star in his own right. His films were low-budget but stood out from the competition because of their detailed story lines and plentiful action.

WAGONMASTER (1950) B/W. *Dir.:* John Ford. *With:* Ben Johnson, Harry Carey, Jr., Ward Bond, Joanne Dru, Jane Darwell, Alan Mowbray. **85 mins.** No rating. Beta, VHS **($N/A).** Nostalgia Merchant. ★★★

A Mormon wagon train headed for Utah (under the leadership of Bond) is joined by two roaming cowboys (Johnson and Carey). On the journey they pick up actors from a traveling medicine show, encounter an outlaw family running from a posse, run afoul of Navajo Indians, and ford a river. This is a pleasant and leisurely production and the leads are appealing. Director Ford wrote the story on which the film was based, and the movie was one of his favorites. It's a lyrical, nostalgic, episodic view of the west, beautifully photographed on location in Utah. However, some viewers may find the film too sentimental and lacking in action. Look for James (*Gunsmoke*) Arness as one of the outlaw brothers, and Jim Thorpe as a Navajo chief. The movie provided the inspiration for the *Wagon Train* TV series, which also starred Bond, reprising his role as the wagonmaster. Ford even directed a few episodes of the show for his long-time friend Bond.

WAGON WHEELS (1934) B/W. *Dir.:* Charles T. Barton. *With:* Randolph Scott, Gail Patrick, Monte Blue, Leila Bennett, Raymond Hatton. **54 mins.** No rating. Beta, VHS **($24.95).** Discount. ★★

In this routine western, Scott plays a wagon-train scout who safely leads settlers through hostile Indian territory to Oregon. The movie was based on Zane Grey's novel *Fighting Caravans*, whose title and story had already been used in a 1931 film starring Gary Cooper. Much leftover footage from the earlier film was used in *Wagon Wheels*, and Scott even wore Cooper's buckskin costume so the shots would match.

WALL STREET COWBOY (1939) B/W. *Dir.:* Joseph Kane. *With:* Roy Rogers, George "Gabby" Hayes, Raymond Hatton, Ann Baldwin, Pierre Watkin. **54 mins.** No rating. Beta, VHS **($24.95).** Discount. ★★

This unassuming early offering from Rogers has him getting mixed up with financial dealings. This was made at a time when Republic was beginning to realize that they had a hot property in Rogers, who in 1939 and the two following years was audiences' third most popular cowboy star—outranked only by Gene Autry and William Boyd. Director Kane, who worked with Rogers on this one, made twenty song-and-action stories with the cowboy star. This is a pleasant example.

WAR OF THE WILDCATS (1943) B/W. *Dir.:* Albert S. Rogell. *With:* John Wayne, Martha Scott, Albert Dekker, George "Gabby" Hayes, Marjorie Rambeau, Dale Evans. **102 mins.** No rating. Beta, VHS **($39.95).** Republic. ★★★

An oil promoter and a quiet cowboy clash on two fronts—they fight over the rights to valuable oil land, and they both want the same woman. At this time Wayne was Republic's hotshot western attraction, making movies for them between starring for larger studios. This spectacular action picture is good A-budget entertainment. Look for Dale Evans in the cast. The title was changed to *In Old Oklahoma* after the opening playdates.

WAR WAGON, THE (1967) C. *Dir.:* Burt Kennedy. *With:* John Wayne, Kirk Douglas, Howard Keel, Robert Walker, Jr., Keenan Wynn, Bruce Cabot, Bruce Dern. **101 mins.** No rating. Beta, VHS **($39.95).** MCA. ★★★★

Ex-con Wayne and the killer hired to shoot him decide to pool their resources and together steal the war wagon of the title—an armored stagecoach equipped with a Gatling gun. In the process Wayne plans to recover gold stolen from him while he was in jail (he was framed). This is a real old-fashioned western—rip-roaring, action-packed entertainment to delight Wayne buffs. Keel makes a fine Indian.

WESTERNER, THE (1940) B/W. *Dir.:* William Wyler. *With:* Gary Cooper, Walter Brennan, Doris Davenport, Fred Stone, Dana Andrews, Forrest Tucker, Chill Wills. **100 mins.** No rating. Beta, VHS **($39.95).** Embassy. ★★★★

This great western character study explodes into full-blooded action when violence erupts over a land dispute. Drifter Cole Hardin (Cooper, in true laconic form) is up before Judge Roy Bean on a horse-stealing charge and his fate looks grim—until he discovers the judge's infatuation with entertainer Lillie Langtry. The quick-thinking Cole fabricates a friendship with Lillie, and the judge sets him free on the understanding that he'll get a lock of the lady's hair and give it to the judge. Cole does arrange a meeting between Bean and the beautiful Lillie, but not quite the way either of the men envisaged it. Cooper is great here, and Brennan's equally fine performance won a well-deserved Best Supporting Actor Oscar (Brennan's third). All-around good entertainment, well worth its status as a genre classic. Good performances, too, from Forrest Tucker and Dana Andrews, both making their first screen appearances.

The Westerner

WEST OF THE DIVIDE (1934) B/W. *Dir.:* Robert N. Bradbury. *With:* John Wayne, George "Gabby" Hayes, Virginia Brown Faire, Yakima Canutt. **60 mins.** No rating. Beta, VHS **($19.95).** Kartes, Sony, Spotlite. ★★★

This typical early thirties Wayne vehicle sends our hero on a hunt for a killer. He plays a cowboy who returns to his childhood home to learn that his father has been murdered and his kid brother, who was home when the crime occurred, has vanished. This entertaining early Monogram entry features Wayne in fine form, and there's a terrific sequence in which Canutt dives from a galloping horse through a closed window. (Sony's tapes are in Beta Hi-Fi and VHS Hi-Fi.)

WEST OF THE LAW (1942) B/W. *Dir.:* Howard Bretherton. *With:* Buck Jones, Tim McCoy, Raymond Hatton, Evelyn Cook, Harry Woods. **60 mins.** No rating. Beta, VHS **($24.95).** Discount. ★★½

This tale in the "Rough Riders" series has McCoy as a minister and Hatton as an undertaker helping good guy Jones track down baddies who have hijacked a gold shipment. It's lots of fun. The three leads look good together.

West of the Law

Wilderness Mail

WESTWARD HO (1935) B/W. *Dir.:* Robert N. Bradbury. *With:* John Wayne, Sheila Mannors, Frank McGlynn, Jr., Jack Curtis, Yakima Canutt. **55 mins.** No rating. Beta, VHS **($N/A).** Video Connection. ★★★½

Wayne is a cowboy whose brother turns out to be the brains behind a villainous outlaw gang—a familiar plot used in one form or another in many low-budget westerns of the thirties. Despite the familiarity, however, this is a superior western. It is a large-scale production with a strong cast and plenty of action. This was Wayne's first B-picture for Republic, and as his popularity grew, the quality of his pictures improved. Wayne also began to project a new image of the cowboy, injecting a bit of fallibility into the pure-as-the-driven-snow persona of the great cowboys of the day. Wayne wanted to get away from these "too goddam perfect" stars of the twenties and thirties and said he wanted to play the sort of hero who "fights clean whenever possible but will fight dirty if he has to."

WILD BUNCH, THE (1969) C. *Dir.:* Sam Peckinpah. *With:* William Holden, Ernest Borgnine, Robert Ryan, Edmond O'Brien, Warren Oates, Ben Johnson, Strother Martin, Jaime Sanchez, L.Q. Jones. **127 mins.** (tapes); **145 mins.** (discs). Rated R. Beta, VHS **($64.95);** Laser **($39.98);** CED **($29.98).** Warner. ★★★★

On release *The Wild Bunch* unleashed an avalanche of critical reaction, which veered wildly from passionate praise for its power and energy to loathing of what some viewed as its gratuitous violence—*Newsday*'s Joseph Gelmis called it "the bloodiest movie I've ever seen, maybe the bloodiest ever made." Director Peckinpah himself claimed that his intention was to turn viewers away from violence by making a picture that thoroughly deglamorized it. So, for starters, this is not for the squeamish, who should know enough by now to stay away from any film with Peckinpah's directorial credit on it. However, many viewers with stronger stomachs complain that heavy cutting by the studio diluted Peckinpah's message and obscured the relationships of the characters—the director's own final cut ran 144 minutes. The story concerns a group of aging outlaws, led by Pike Bishop (Holden), who escape into Mexico and are forced to agree to help vicious anti-revolutionary Mapache rob an army supply train. When Mapache learns that the youngest of the bunch, Angel (Sanchez), is a revolutionary, he tortures him. Angel's plight forces the other four to review their cold-hearted attitudes and go to his rescue. Whatever your views on the violence involved, this is exciting, and ultimately moving, cinema.

WILDERNESS MAIL (1935) B/W. *Dir.:* Forrest Sheldon. *With:* Kermit Maynard, Fred Kohler, Doris Brook, Dick Curtis, Syd Saylor, Paul Hurst. **65 mins.** No rating. Beta, VHS **($N/A).** Video Connection ★★

One of a string of cheapies Maynard made for Ambassador in the mid-thirties, with enough action and excitement to keep viewers involved. This series was one of numerous mini-budget series being churned out at the time, and probably one of the best. Kermit had won the World's Champion Trick Riding and Fancy Riding contests in competition in 1931 and 1933, and his skill on horseback made for some exciting stunting and trick riding in his films.

WILD FRONTIER, THE (1947) B/W. *Di*
Allan "Rocky" Lane, Jack Holt, Eddy W
John James, Roy Barcroft. **59 mins.** No rating. Beta, VHS **($24.95).** Discount. ★★★

An above-average actioner with Lane coming to the aid of an old lawman who is trying to tame a frontier town. This was the first of Lane's long-running Republic series. The movies were cheaply made, but usually well-plotted, suspenseful, and big on action. Lane is in good form here, and he gets superior support from Holt. A good bet for B-western fans.

The Wild Frontier

Wild Horse

WILD HORSE (1931) B/W. *Dir.:* Richard Thorpe and Sidney Algier. *With:* Hoot Gibson, Alberta Vaughn, Stepin Fetchit. **68 mins.** No rating. Beta, VHS **($49.95).** Video Yesteryear. ★★

One of Hoot's own favorite sound films, this one really stars Gibson's gorgeous palomino. The story is about attempts to capture the horse. The comedy is provided by black actor Fetchit, who would later be accused of fostering racial stereotypes with his "Yassuh" performances. Gibson is his amiable self, but by the time this movie was released his star was on the wane. The film is an interesting oddity for B-movie historians and, of course, horse lovers.

WILD HORSE CANYON (1938) B/W. *Dir.:* Robert Hill. *With:* Jack Randall, Dorothy Short, Frank Yaconelli, Dennis Moore, Warner Richmond, Charles King. **56 mins.** No rating. Beta, VHS **($24.95).** Discount. ★★

One of Randall's not-very-successful series for Monogram

(it was dropped for the 1940-41 season). The movie offers tolerable viewing, but don't look for much in the way of thrills. For Randall fans.

WILD HORSE RODEO (1937) B/W. *Dir.:* George Sherman. *With:* Ray Corrigan, Bob Livingston, Max Terhune, June Martel, Walter Miller. **53 mins.** No rating. Beta, VHS **($24.95).** Discount. ★★★

Red Rock Canyon provides the stunning scenery for this fast-moving "Three Mesquiteers" production. Dick Weston—soon to become famous as Roy Rogers—has a bit part singing in a cantina. Lots of great action. This was the first film Livingston made after suffering a skull fracture that kept him out of *The Trigger Trio* (see review), in which he was replaced by Ralph Byrd, star of Republic's "Dick Tracy" serials. Livingston recovered from his injury and made this and five other films in the series.

WILD MUSTANG (1935) B/W. *Dir.:* Harry Fraser. *With:* Harry Carey, Barbara Fritchie, Del Gordon, Cathryn Jons, Robert Kortman. **42 mins.** No rating. Beta, VHS **($24.95).** Discount. ★★

The good guy and the bad guy happen to be brothers in this cheapie about the taming of a horse. This flick was released by a mini-budget independent company called Ajax and stars the popular Harry Carey, who became an unsuccessful playwright and then an actor after a bout of pneumonia interrupted his law studies. Success in westerns came late to Carey—he was almost forty when Universal signed him in 1915.

WINNING OF THE WEST (1953) B/W. *Dir.:* George Archainbaud. *With:* Gene Autry, Smiley Burnette, Gail Davis, Richard Crane, Robert Livingston. **57 mins.** No rating. Beta, VHS **($34.95).** Blackhawk. ★★★

Ranger Autry is under orders to protect a crusading newspaper publisher and his printer (Burnette) from unscrupulous crooks who use Indian raids to cover up their own nefarious activities. Then the hero's outlaw brother kills the publisher. This is a solid actioner from Columbia with plenty of interest value for Autry fans. Songs include "Cowboy Blues" and "Five Minutes Late and a Dollar Short." *Winning of the West* is also available on a double bill with *Melody Trail* from Republic for $39.95.

YELLOW ROSE OF TEXAS, THE (1944) B/W. *Dir.:* Joseph Kane. *With:* Roy Rogers, Dale Evans, George Cleveland, Harry Shannon, Grant Withers, Bob Nolan and the Sons of the Pioneers. **55 mins.** No rating. Beta, VHS **($39.95).** Video Yesteryear. ★★★

High-quality entertainment from Rogers and his entourage, made at a time when Rogers himself was riding high in the popularity polls and studio bosses were pulling out all the stops to keep him there. In this tale Rogers joins a river showboat as part of a plan to recover stolen money. (The plot is somewhat similar to that of Gene Autry's 1941 release *Ridin' on a Rainbow*.) The Sons of the Pioneers get in some good songs.

YOUNG BILL HICKOK (1940) B/W. *Dir.:* Joseph Kane. *With:* Roy Rogers, George "Gabby" Hayes, Jacqueline Wells, John Miljan, Sally Payne, Monte Blue. **59 mins.** No rating. Beta, VHS **($24.95).** Discount. ★★

A slight and only mildly entertaining "historical" western from Rogers' early period, with Payne seriously miscast as Calamity Jane. There are some interesting names in the cast, but for anyone who's hungering for a Rogers movie, there are better choices than this.

YOUNG BLOOD (1932) B/W. *Dir.:* Phil Rosen. *With:* Bob Steele, Helen Foster, Naomi Judge, Charles King. **59 mins.** No rating. Beta, VHS **($24.95).** Discount. ★★

An early outing for Bob Steele, who had made his sound debut two years earlier for Tiffany in *Near the Rainbow's End*. He made this one for Monogram when his popularity, inspired by his remarkable good looks and better-than-average acting skills, was on the rise. It's easy to see the attraction in this routine but enjoyable film.

YOUNG BUFFALO BILL (1940) B/W. *Dir.:* Joseph Kane. *With:* Roy Rogers, George "Gabby" Hayes, Pauline Moore, Hugh Sothern, Chief Thunder Cloud. **59 mins.** No rating. Beta, VHS **($24.95).** Discount. ★★

Another of Rogers' low-budget "historical" tales. This one attempts to cash in on a legend of the Old West with only middling results. It's reasonably entertaining and the cast tries hard, but it's a lackluster product for all that.

DIRECTORY OF VIDEO SUPPLIERS

Blackhawk Films & Video Corp.
1235 West Fifth
Box 3990
Davenport, IA 52808

Buena Vista Home Video
500 South Buena Vista Street
Burbank, CA 91521

CBS/Fox Video
1211 Avenue of the Americas
New York, NY 10036

Continental Video
2320 Cotner
Los Angeles, CA 90064

Crown Video
Publisher's Central Bureau
Dept. 321
1 Champion Avenue
Avenel, NJ 07001

Discount Video Tapes Inc.
3711B West Clark Avenue
PO Box 7122
Burbank, CA 91510

Embassy Home Entertainment
1901 Avenue of the Stars
Los Angeles, CA 90067

Hollywood Home Theater
4590 Santa Monica Blvd.
Los Angeles, CA 90029

Independent United Distributors
430 West 54th Street
New York, NY 10019

Kartes Productions Inc.
10 East 106th Street
Indianapolis, IN 46280

Key Video
1211 Avenue of the Americas
New York, NY 10036

Maljack Productions, Inc.
15825 Rob Roy Drive
Oak Forest, IL 60452

MCA Home Video
70 Universal City Plaza
Universal City, CA 91608

Media Home Entertainment, Inc.
5730 Buckingham Parkway
Culver City, CA 90230

MGM/UA Home Video
1350 Avenue of the Americas
New York, NY 10019

New World Video
1888 Century Park East
Los Angeles, CA 90067

Nostalgia Merchant
Media Home Entertainment, Inc.
5730 Buckingham Parkway
Culver City, CA 90230

Paramount Home Video
5555 Melrose Avenue
Los Angeles, CA 90038

Prism Entertainment
1875 Century Park East
Suite 1010
Los Angeles, CA 90067

RCA/Columbia Home Video
2901 W. Alameda
Burbank, CA 91505

Republic Pictures Home Video
12636 Beatrice Street
PO Box 66930
Los Angeles, CA 90066-0930

RKO HomeVideo
15840 Ventura Boulevard
Suite 303
Encino, CA 91436

Sagebrush Productions
1940 S. Cotner Avenue
Los Angeles, CA 90025

Sony Corporation of America
Video Software Operations
9 West 57th Street
New York, NY 10019

Spotlite Video
Republic Pictures Home Video
12636 Beatrice Street
PO Box 66930
Los Angeles, CA 90066-0930

Thorn EMI/Home Box Office Video Inc.
1370 Avenue of the Americas
New York, NY 10019

United Entertainment Inc.
6535 East Skelly Drive
Tulsa, OK 74145

Vestron Video
1011 High Ridge Road
PO Box 4000
Stamford, CT 06907

VidAmerica Inc.
235 East 55th Street
New York, NY 10022

Video Connection/Cassette Express
3123 Sylvania Avenue
Toledo, OH 43613

Video Dimensions
110 East 23rd Street
Suite 603
New York, NY 10010

Video Gems
731 North La Brea Avenue
PO Box 38188
Los Angeles, CA 90038

Video Yesteryear
Box C
Sandy Hook, CT 06482

Warner Home Video, Inc.
4000 Warner Blvd.
Burbank, CA 91522